MODERN PUBLISHING'S

IS THAT YOUR FINAL ANSWER?

VOLUME 1

MODERN PUBLISHING
A Division of Unisystems, Inc.
New York, New York 10022
Series UPC: 39850

In *Is That Your Final Answer?*, trivia buffs will find hundreds of questions to test their knowledge of history, science, literature, art, sports, movies, music, and many more topics. Challenging and fun, the questions in *Is That Your Final Answer?* will show you just how much you know, and how much you don't know! Whether you enjoy these brain-teasing questions on your own or with a group of friends, *Is That Your Final Answer?* is a must for anyone who loves facts, figures, history, and a good challenge. And when you are through with *Is That Your Final Answer? Volume 1*, you'll find more stimulating trivia questions in *Is That Your Final Answer? Volume 2*. No trivia buff should be without them.

1.

Which state's motto is "Live Free or Die"?
a) Pennsylvania
b) Connecticut
c) Massachusetts
d) New Hampshire

2.

Walt Disney was the creator of which popular animated cartoon character?
a) Betty Boop
b) Bugs Bunny
c) Garfield
d) Mickey Mouse

3.

Who was the first woman to fly across the Atlantic Ocean alone?
a) Elizabeth Cady Stanton
b) Amelia Earhart
c) Marie Curie
d) Margaret Mitchell

4.

In which popular game is the object to score more runs than your opponent over the course of nine innings?
a) baseball
b) soccer
c) football
d) golf

5.

Who is the Carthaginian leader known for crossing the Italian Alps with elephants and for nearly taking over Rome—a feat that would have changed the course of the history of the world?

a) Hannibal
b) Genghis Khan
c) Marco Polo
d) Attila the Hun

6.

What is the phenomenon of the earth's plates pushing violently against one another called?

a) typhoon
b) earthquake
c) avalanche
d) squall

7.

Who was a legendary peace officer of the Old West?

a) George A. Custer
b) Davy Crockett
c) William Cody
d) Wyatt Earp

8.

Which ill-fated love affair involved a brilliant Roman soldier and a queen of Egypt?

a) Antony and Cleopatra
b) Romeo and Juliet
c) Pocahontas and John Smith
d) none of the above

9.

Which three are popularly known as "The Three Tenors"?
a) Pavarotti
b) Domingo
c) Caruso
d) Carrera

10.

Which is the national symbol of the U.S.?
a) the Condor
b) the golden eagle
c) the bald eagle
d) the carrier pigeon

11.

Which is not a letter from the Hebrew alphabet?
a) omega
b) gemel
c) tet
d) yod

12.

In which period of literature were the great novels
David Copperfield, War and Peace, and *Adventures of
Huckleberry Finn* written?
a) Age of Reason
b) Romanticism
c) Modern Age
d) Realism

13.

Who was known as "The Wizard of Menlo Park"?
a) Alexander Graham Bell
b) Thomas Edison
c) Pierre Curie
d) Jonas Salk

14.

In Alfred Hitchcock's movie *North by Northwest*, who was Cary Grant saving from James Mason?
a) Bette Davis
b) Doris Day
c) Grace Kelly
d) Eva Marie Saint

15.

Whose song "Take the A Train" was one of the best-selling songs of the 1930s?
a) Fats Domino
b) Benny Goodman
c) Glenn Miller
d) Duke Ellington

16.

Where is the Everglades National Park?
a) Texas
b) Florida
c) Mexico
d) Louisiana

17.

Which baseball team won the World Series four times in a row from 1936 to 1939?
a) New York Yankees
b) St. Louis Cardinals
c) Cincinnati Reds
d) Detroit Tigers

18.

What is the center of the circulatory system of the human body?
a) the brain
b) the heart
c) the lungs
d) the stomach

19.

Where did Ponce de Leon go to find the Fountain of Youth?
a) Florida
b) Puerto Rico
c) Virgin Islands
d) Aruba

20.

Which body of water is on the west coast of the Florida peninsula?
a) Pacific Ocean
b) Gulf of Mexico
c) Atlantic Ocean
d) Caribbean Sea

21.

Who was Virginia Dare?
a) the first baby born in America to English parents in 1587
b) a women's rights advocate
c) the founder of the first school for nursing
d) the first woman to cross the Atlantic Ocean in a
   vessel alone

22.

What is Fort Knox best known as?
a) the home of the U.S. Treasury Department's gold depository
b) as a large army base
c) as an army training base
d) all of the above

23.

What is the name of the spaceship John H. Glenn was in when he became the first American to orbit earth?
a) Friendship 7
b) Gemini
c) Apollo
d) Voyager

24.

What is the center of the nervous system of the human body?
a) the brain
b) the spinal cord
c) neurons
d) none of the above

25.

According to proper etiquette, how would you address the president of the U.S. if you met him in person?
a) by his surname
b) by his given name
c) Mr. President
d) Your Honor

26.

What is the most widely known book in the English-speaking world?
a) the Bible
b) *Gone with the Wind*
c) the Koran
d) the Torah

27.

Which hockey legend retired in 1999?
a) Mark Messier
b) Phil Esposito
c) Mario Lemieux
d) Wayne Gretzky

28.

Where, in 1692, were 19 people executed for "witchcraft"?
a) Salem, Massachusetts
b) New York City, New York
c) Boston, Massachusetts
d) Williamsburg, Virginia

29.

For which movie did Clark Gable win an Academy Award in 1934?

a) *The Misfits*
b) *Gone with the Wind*
c) *It Happened One Night*
d) *Strange Cargo*

30.

Whose speech—the Gettysburg Address—closed with the following, "...that government of the people, by the people, for the people, shall not perish from the earth"?

a) Thomas Jefferson
b) Abraham Lincoln
c) George Washington
d) none of the above

31.

What is a spring that gushes hot water and steam into the air called?

a) waterfall
b) geyser
c) sauna
d) whirlpool

32.

Which singer from a popular group reprised the song "I Only Have Eyes for You" on his solo album?

a) Smokey Robinson
b) Art Garfunkle
c) Little Richard
d) Neil Diamond

33.

Where did the Boston Tea Party take place?
a) Boston Harbor
b) Boston Commons
c) Fanieul Hall
d) Harvard Square

34.

Who was Oscar Hammerstein II's best-known collaborator?
a) Jerome Kern
b) Richard Rogers
c) Sigmund Romberg
d) George Gershwin

35.

Of those listed, which is the smallest bird?
a) parakeet
b) hummingbird
c) finch
d) none of the above

36.

Which event took place in 1775?
a) George Washington was named commander-in-chief
b) Ben Franklin invented the lightning rod
c) Henry Hudson made his first voyage
d) the French and Indian War came to an end

37.

Where did the Industrial Revolution first take place?
a) Spain
b) France
c) England
d) United States

38.

Where is Independence Hall—considered by many to be the birthplace of the U.S.?
a) Boston
b) Philadelphia
c) Dallas
d) Williamsburg

39.

Who was Jesse James?
a) a civil rights activist
b) a famous outlaw
c) an olympic champion
d) a linebacker

40.

Which landmark 1966 Supreme Court case stated that a suspect must be read his rights before being questioned?
a) Schenck v. U.S.
b) Miranda v. Arizona
c) Muller v. Oregon
d) Roth v. U.S.

41.

Which baseball team won the World Series five times in a row from 1950 to 1954?
a) New York Yankees
b) Oakland Athletics
c) Minnesota Twins
d) Brooklyn Dodgers

42.

In which popular game is the object to score points by shooting or sinking a ball through a basket?
a) basketball
b) volleyball
c) tennis
d) bowling

43.

Who was the first vice president of the U.S.?
a) John Adams
b) Thomas Jefferson
c) Aaron Burr
d) Chester A. Arthur

44.

Which of these events happened in 1640?
a) the first theater opened in Williamsburg, Virginia
b) Roger Williams founded Providence, Rhode Island
c) Captain Kidd settled in America
d) the first book was printed in America

45.

Who did Tiny Tim—the ukelele-toting singer—marry on TV?
a) Miss Piggy
b) Miss Burns
c) Miss Brooks
d) Miss Vicki

46.

Is Genesis
a) a pop rock band
b) a book from the Bible
c) a word that means "beginning"
d) all of the above

47.

Who won the Men's Wimbledon Championship five times in a row from 1976 to 1980?
a) Bjørn Borg
b) John McEnroe
c) Boris Becker
d) Jimmy Conners

48.

What are Go Fish, Solitaire, and War?
a) names of Emmy-winning TV shows
b) rock bands
c) popular card games
d) none of the above

49.

Which female tennis star ranked #1 for a record-breaking 377 weeks before retiring in 1999?

a) Steffi Graf

b) Martina Hingis

c) Serena Williams

d) none of the above

50.

What part of the human body helps it to move?

a) muscles

b) digestive system

c) circulatory system

d) none of the above

51.

Which indoor sport attracts more participants than any other indoor sport?

a) bowling

b) table tennis

c) darts

d) none of the above

52.

Without this feature of anatomy, humans would not be able to hold themselves upright

a) skeleton

b) circulatory system

c) digestive system

d) alimentary system

53.

In the movie *How To Marry a Millionaire*, who was not one of the stars?
a) Bette Davis
b) Marilyn Monroe
c) Lauren Bacall
d) Betty Grable

54.

What order of mammals do koalas fall into?
a) marsupialia
b) primates
c) carnivora
d) insectivora

55.

Which of these famous works of literature was published first?
a) *Leaves of Grass*
b) *Moby Dick*
c) *The Great Gatsby*
d) *A Clockwork Orange*

56.

What kind of court handles matters dealing with youth offenders?
a) juvenile
b) federal
c) Supeme Court
d) none

57.

Who was the top-scoring champion in basketball for six years in a row from 1987 to 1992?
a) Michael Jordan
b) Dennis Rodman
c) Patrick Ewing
d) Kareem Abdul-Jabbar

58.

In which Supreme Court case was it ruled that state anti-abortion laws were unconstitutional?
a) Roe v. Wade
b) Baker v. Carr
c) Bower v. Hardwich
d) none of the above

59.

Who was Janet Guthrie?
a) the first woman to race in the Indianapolis 500
b) the first woman in space
c) the first woman governor in the U.S.
d) the first woman to climb Mount Everest

60.

In 1896, where were the first modern Olympics held?
a) France
b) United States
c) Greece
d) Germany

61.

How many songs are on the Duets II album by
Frank Sinatra?
a) 11
b) 13
c) 14
d) 15

62.

When Theodore Roosevelt was the president, who was
vice president?
a) Calvin Coolidge
b) Adlai E. Stevenson
c) Charles W. Fairbanks
d) none of the above

63.

Who was the first woman to run the Boston Marathon
and did so in 1972 disguised as a man?
a) Greta Weiss
b) Kathrine Switzer
c) Florence Griffith Joyner
d) Sonia O'Sullivan

64.

Which of these events happened in 1636?
a) Plymouth Colony was founded
b) Pocahontas traveled to England
c) Roger Williams founded Providence, Rhode Island
d) all of the above

65.

Which has the greatest noise level in decibels?
a) jet engine
b) jackhammer
c) diesel truck
d) a dog barking

66.

What does melanin control in the body?
a) the color of the skin
b) blood pressure
c) cholesterol levels
d) liver function

67.

Who do the eating disorders anorexia nervosa and bulimia affect most often?
a) young males
b) teenage girls
c) senior citizens
d) toddlers

68.

Who was Bill Beutel's long-time co-host on a news program in the 1960s?
a) Lehrer
b) Donaldson
c) Grimsby
d) Walters

69.

Which is the last letter of the Greek alphabet?
a) beta
b) alpha
c) omega
d) iota

70.

Who was the Women's Wimbledon Champion in 1966?
a) Billie Jean King
b) Martina Navratilova
c) Steffi Graf
d) Chris Evert

71.

Where would you find the "Tree of Knowledge" and
the "Tree of Life"?
a) Disneyland
b) the Garden of Eden
c) Sesame Street
d) none of the above

72.

Where did Noah's Ark supposedly come to rest after
the flood?
a) Mount Olympus
b) Mount McKinley
c) Mount Ararat
d) Mount Everest

73.

Which is not one of the five senses?
a) sight
b) touch
c) smell
d) speech

74.

In 1849, what was the mass migration of prospectors looking for gold called?
a) the Gold Rush
b) the Westward Movement
c) Manifest Destiny
d) none of the above

75.

Who painted *The Last Supper*?
a) Leonardo da Vinci
b) Michelangelo
c) Raphael
d) Bellini

76.

Which event happened in 1776?
a) Ben Franklin invented bifocal lenses
b) George Washington was elected the first president of the U.S.
c) The Declaration of Independence was approved
d) none of the above

77.

In which movie did John Wayne find Natalie Wood living amongst the Comanche?
a) *True Grit*
b) *The Searchers*
c) *The Way We Were*
d) *To Sir With Love*

78.

Who was one of the leading figures of the Pop Art Movement in the 1960s?
a) Andy Warhol
b) Thomas Sully
c) Roy Lichtenstein
d) Andrew Wyeth

79.

Which French painter developed the technique known as pointillism?
a) Renoir
b) Monet
c) Manet
d) Seurat

80.

During which decade did people do the dance called the Stroll?
a) 1940s
b) 1950s
c) 1960s
d) 1970s

81.

For which state are the letters MI an abbreviation?
a) Michigan
b) Minnesota
c) Missouri
d) Mississippi

82.

Can you define the word oxymoron?
a) a dumb ox
b) a pair of contradictory words
c) a chemical element
d) a layer of the earth's atmosphere

83.

Which is not an oxymoron?
a) almost perfect
b) definite maybe
c) instant classic
d) a drop in the bucket

84.

Which book by Jack Kerouac was published in 1957?
a) *On the Road*
b) *The Town and the City*
c) *The Dharma Bums*
d) *Big Sur*

85.

Who composed the music for *The William Tell Overture*?
a) Mozart
b) Rossini
c) Bernstein
d) Bach

86.

Finish this beatitude: Blessed are the meek for they...
a) shall inherit the earth
b) shall be saved
c) shall walk through the Valley of Death
d) shall sit at the right hand of God

87.

Who immortalized the amazing feat of David in a
marble sculpture?
a) Leonardo da Vinci
b) Michelangelo
c) Vincent van Gogh
d) Raphael

88.

Does the Golden Rule refer to
a) an ethical teaching
b) a retirement plan
c) a mutual fund
d) none of the above

89.

Where is the Little Big Horn Battlefield National Park?
a) Montana
b) South Dakota
c) North Dakota
d) Wyoming

90.

Which state's motto is, "United we stand, divided we fall"?
a) Alabama
b) Pennsylvania
c) Kentucky
d) Massachusetts

91.

Mexican artist, Diego Rivera, is best known as
a) a sculptor
b) a muralist
c) a portraitist
d) a caricaturist

92.

Which is not an architectural term denoting a style from a certain time period?
a) Corinthian
b) Renaissance
c) Romanesque
d) Norman

93.

When was the Jitterbug a popular dance?
a) 1920s
b) 1930s
c) 1940s
d) 1950s

94.

What does the Greek prefix pyro- mean?
a) fire
b) wing
c) mind
d) false

95.

During which period of literature were *Leaves of Grass* and *A Doll's House* written?
a) Realism
b) Romanticism
c) Modern Age
d) Age of Reason

96.

What was the name of the fist atomic-powered submarine, which was launched in 1954?
a) Nautilus
b) Alvin
c) Red October
d) none of the above

97.

In *Casablanca,* who played the freedom fighter who competed with Rick for Ilsa's love?
a) Humphrey Bogart
b) Paul Henreid
c) Peter Lorre
d) William Holden

98.

In the rhyme "Baa baa black sheep," where did the little boy who was to receive a bag of wool live?
a) down the lane
b) up the street
c) around the corner
d) in the hood

99.

What does the Greek prefix aero- mean?
a) air, gas
b) fly
c) sing
d) none of the above

100.

Which period of literature deals with disillusioned characters and takes an introspective look at social conditions?
a) Realism
b) Modern Age
c) Romanticism
d) the Age of Reason

101.

Which became the 50th state of the U.S.?
a) Kentucky
b) Hawaii
c) Massachusetts
d) Pennsylvania

102.

In 1876, where was General George Custer defeated by Sioux warriors?
a) Little Big Horn
b) Cumberland Gap
c) Gettysburg
d) Washita Battlefield

103.

For which organization was the Niagara Movement—begun in 1905—originally the name?
a) NATO
b) NAACP
c) WPA
d) none of the above

104.

Who was Nellie Ross Taylor, a woman from Wyoming?
a) the first woman governor in the U.S. in 1925
b) a suffragette
c) a leader of the Civil Rights Movement
d) designer of the first U.S. flag

105.

Who was the first African-American woman elected to Congress?
a) Shirley Chisholm
b) Marian Anderson
c) Harriet Beecher Stowe
d) Billie Holiday

106.

In which year did two players break the season record set by Roger Maris for number of home runs in a season?
a) 1996
b) 1997
c) 1998
d) 1999

107.

What treatment helps to keep you immune from diseases like typhoid fever, smallpox, and tuberculosis?
a) vaccines
b) aspirins
c) antibiotics
d) heat packs

108.

Where was the first permanent English settlement established in America?
a) Jamestown, Virginia
b) Boston, Massachusetts
c) St. Louis, Missouri
d) Philadelphia, Pennsylvania

109.

In 1825, which canal was opened, cutting travel time from New York City to the Great Lakes?
a) Erie Canal
b) Panama Canal
c) Suez Canal
d) none of the above

110.

What do Alistair Simms, George C. Scott, and Patrick Stewart have in common?
a) all played Captain Ahab
b) all played Scrooge
c) all were stars of TV series
d) none of the above

111.

Where is the world's longest free-standing stalactite?
a) Ireland
b) France
c) Spain
d) Ethiopia

112.

What is left of the Cheshire Cat once he disappears?
a) nothing
b) his grin
c) his tail
d) his eyes

113.

What causes a volcano to erupt?
a) magma
b) water
c) ashes
d) none of the above

114.

Which three are famous Portuguese explorers?
a) Vasco da Gama
b) Amerigo Vespucci
c) Ferdinand Magellan
d) Bartholomeu Dias

115.

Which 19th-century writer was best known for macabre tales and poems?
a) Herman Melville
b) Edgar Allan Poe
c) Emily Dickinson
d) Henry James

116.

Which story is one written by beloved author of fairy tales Hans Christian Andersen?
a) Red Riding Hood
b) The Ugly Duckling
c) Ali Baba
d) The Boy Who Cried Wolf

117.

Which is the largest ocean in the world?
a) Pacific
b) Indian
c) Atlantic
d) none of the above

118.

Where is the headquarters of NATO?
a) France
b) Spain
c) Belgium
d) Germany

119.

What kind of shoe did Cinderella lose running from the ball at midnight?
a) ballet slipper
b) running shoe
c) sandal
d) glass slipper

120.

On the *Sleepless in Seattle* soundtrack, how many of the songs are sung by Jimmy Durante?
a) none
b) one
c) two
d) three

121.

Which is the second largest ocean in the world?
a) Pacific
b) Atlantic
c) Indian
d) Arctic

122.

Where is Grand Canyon National Park?
a) Arizona
b) Texas
c) Utah
d) North Dakota

123.

Which of these novels by Ernest Hemingway were made into films?
a) *Farewell to Arms*
b) *To Have and Have Not*
c) *The Sun Also Rises*
d) all of the above

124.

In what capital city of the world is NATO headquartered?
a) Paris
b) Rome
c) Brussels
d) Geneva

125.

In the fairy tale The Three Little Pigs, which house was the first destroyed by the wolf who huffed and puffed and blew the house down?

a) one of bricks
b) one of straw
c) one of wood
d) one of cards

126.

In 1348, which epidemic ravaged Europe?

a) smallpox
b) typhoid fever
c) malaria
d) the Black Death

127.

What event in 1969 started the modern gay rights movement?

a) the Stonewall Rebellion
b) uprisings at Attica
c) the Roe v. Wade Supreme Court decision
d) none of the above

128.

Who was a leader of the Underground Railroad in 1863?

a) Harriet Tubman
b) Rosa Parks
c) Harriet Beecher Stowe
d) Frederick Douglass

129.

Leonardo da Vinci, the most pre-eminent figure of the Renaissance, was known as a
a) painter
b) sculptor
c) engineer
d) all of the above

130.

To which flamboyant pianist is there a museum dedicated in Las Vegas, Nevada?
a) Elton John
b) Bobby Short
c) Liberace
d) Mozart

131.

In 1865, where was the first college for women established in the U.S.?
a) Vassar College
b) Smith College
c) Harvard University
d) none of the above

132.

Who explored the South Pacific in the 1700s?
a) Sir Richard Burton
b) James Cook
c) Leif Erikson
d) Roald Amundsen

133.
Of these early civilizations, which believed the earth was flat?
a) Hindus
b) Egyptians
c) Ancient Babylonians
d) early Europeans

134.
What is a group of rhinoceroses referred to as?
a) herd
b) crash
c) horde
d) gang

135.
Michelangelo, one of the foremost figures of the Renaissance, who sculpted the statue of David, is also famous for painting
a) parts of the Sistine Chapel
b) the Colosseum
c) the Parthenon
d) the Pyramids

136.
Who wrote *The Martian Chronicles* in 1950?
a) Ray Bradbury
b) Isaac Asimov
c) Robert Heinlein
d) Frank Herbert

137.

Who ruled ancient Egypt?
a) a pharaoh
b) a president
c) a shah
d) a chief

138.

In the Old Testament, which sea parted so Moses could lead the Israelites to freedom?
a) the Sea of Galilee
b) the Black Sea
c) the Red Sea
d) the Caspian Sea

139.

Which book, written by Ernest Hemingway, was made into a movie starring Spencer Tracy?
a) *The Sun Also Rises*
b) *A Farewell to Arms*
c) *The Old Man and the Sea*
d) *To Have and Have Not*

140.

Which holiday in the U.S. is usually celebrated on the second Sunday of May?
a) Citizenship Day
b) Father's Day
c) Flag Day
d) Mother's Day

141.

Are Faith, Hope, and Charity known as
a) great virtues
b) a vaudeville act
c) a TV show
d) none of the above

142.

In the movie *The Third Man*, who did Joseph Cotten pursue?
a) Sydney Greenstreet
b) Orson Welles
c) Robert Redford
d) James Stewart

143.

For which newspaper did Carl Bernstein and Bob Woodward work when they uncovered the Watergate break-in?
a) *Saturday Evening Post*
b) *Washington Post*
c) *New York Times*
d) *USA Today*

144.

What does .mil designate on the Internet?
a) a shopping network
b) a social club
c) a military organization
d) none of the above

145.

What is a group of turtles referred to as?
a) bale
b) band
c) brood
d) drove

146.

Which holiday in the U.S. is usually celebrated on the fourth Thursday of November?
a) Thanksgiving Day
b) Christmas Day
c) New Year's Day
d) Flag Day

147.

Which book of the New Testament are the Four Horsemen from?
a) Genesis
b) Revelation
c) Numbers
d) Psalms

148.

Which is the classic story of a great white whale and an obsessed sea captain?
a) *Jonah*
b) *Moby Dick*
c) *Jaws*
d) *The Deep*

149.

Who sang the popular song "The Circle of Life" in Disney's hit movie *The Lion King?*
a) Celine Dion
b) Barbra Streisand
c) Elton John
d) James Taylor

150.

Dr. Sally Ride became famous because she
a) was the first woman astronaut to travel in space
b) discovered radium
c) wrote a Nobel Prize-winning book
d) none of the above

151.

What is the name Methuselah associated with?
a) wisdom
b) prosperity
c) age
d) commerce

152.

With which group did Grace Slick perform in the 1960s?
a) Jefferson Starship
b) the Mamas and the Papas
c) Jefferson Airplane
d) ABBA

153.

Who was not a painter during the Renaissance period?
a) Michelangelo
b) da Vinci
c) Warhol
d) Raphael

154.

Who wrote the Gospels?
a) Matthew, Mark, Luke, and John
b) Matthew, Mark Michael, and James
c) Matthew, Mark, Paul, and Simon
d) Matthew, Mark, Peter, and Paul

155.

What does Jerusalem mean?
a) City of Peace
b) City of Brotherly Love
c) City of Lights
d) City of Songs

156.

What does .int designate on the Internet?
a) an investment agency
b) a chat group
c) the Internal Revenue Service
d) an international organization

157.

In Internet lingo, what does J/K stand for?
a) left of center
b) the jury is still out
c) just kidding
d) you've crashed

158.

Which art movement was Salvador Dali
associated with?
a) Impressionism
b) Modernism
c) Surrealism
d) Cubism

159.

Who wrote the lyrics to the song "Smile"?
a) Groucho Marx
b) Charlie Chaplin
c) Paul Anka
d) Nick Ashford

160.

In Internet lingo, what does BTW stand for?
a) best on the Web
b) by the way
c) waiting for a reply
d) up to date

161.

Who was the first woman justice on the U.S. Supreme Court?
a) Eleanor Roosevelt
b) Sandra Day O'Connor
c) Ruth Ginsburg
d) Geraldine Ferraro

162.

Which are architectural terms that denote a style from a certain time period?
a) Baroque
b) Ionic
c) Georgian
d) Gothic

163.

What is the equivalent of 1000 in Roman numerals?
a) D
b) L
c) M
d) C

164.

In 1993, who became the first woman Attorney General of the U.S.?
a) Shirley Chisholm
b) Ruth Ginsburg
c) Janet Reno
d) Hillary Clinton

165.

How many of the ten wars fought by the U.S. took place before 1939?

a) 6
b) 5
c) 7
d) 4

166.

Which two states were the next added to the stars and stripes, after the original 13 colonies?

a) Vermont and Kentucky
b) Alabama and Maine
c) North Dakota and South Dakota
d) New Mexico and Arizona

167.

What are the Magellanic Clouds?

a) the galaxies believed to be nearest to the Milky Way
b) the layer of dust particles that surrounds earth in its outer atmosphere
c) the star closest to the sun
d) none of the above

168.

Where is the world's deepest cave?

a) United States
b) France
c) Spain
d) Germany

169.

Which painting is Georgia O'Keeffe known for?
a) *Gloucester*
b) *American Gothic*
c) *Cow's Skull*
d) *Whistler's Mother*

170.

Where are the pyramids?
a) Easter Island
b) Egypt
c) Colombia
d) none of the above

171.

Which two are considered to be signs of peace?
a) an olive branch
b) a shamrock
c) a dove
d) a fig leaf

172.

What does .org designate on the Internet?
a) an organ donor agency
b) a non-profit organization
c) an association for keyboard players
d) an international organization

173.

Analytical, applied, and physical are specialties of the study of which science?

a) chemistry
b) physics
c) mathematics
d) geology

174.

Where were marbles invented circa 3000 BC?

a) Egypt
b) China
c) Europe
d) the Americas

175.

Which of these prefixes are derived from Latin?

a) alti-
b) cerebro-
c) demi-
d) proto-

176.

Which author was not from the period of literature known as Romanticism?

a) Walter Scott
b) Charlotte Brontë
c) Edgar Allan Poe
d) Walt Whitman

177.

Circa 2000 BC, where were kites invented?
a) China
b) India
c) England
d) Mesopotamia

178.

In Internet lingo, what does TTFN stand for?
a) an international coding device
b) a frequency
c) ta ta for now
d) a Web application

179.

In tropical rain forests, what are the lush foliage, vines, and treetops most commonly referred to as?
a) canopy
b) hood
c) cover
d) blanket

180.

What was James Stewart's profession in the movie *Rear Window*?
a) photojournalist
b) lawyer
c) designer
d) architect

181.

What is the Biblical name Job associated with?
a) patience
b) wisdom
c) knowledge
d) prosperity

182.

Little Women is a novel written by
a) Margaret Atwood
b) Margaret Mitchell
c) Louisa May Alcott
d) Pearl Buck

183.

Which of these presidents is *not* portrayed on Mount Rushmore?
a) Washington
b) Lincoln
c) Adams
d) Jefferson

184.

Which is the largest continent in the world?
a) Asia
b) South America
c) Africa
d) India

185.

Which ocean surrounds Africa to the east?
a) Atlantic
b) Indian
c) Pacific
d) Arctic

186.

In Internet lingo, what does FYI stand for?
a) for your investigation
b) forget your instincts
c) for your information
d) none of the above

187.

What is the state motto of California?
a) Eureka!
b) Aloha
c) Big Apple
d) none of the above

188.

When Delilah cut his hair, what did Samson lose?
a) strength
b) courage
c) knowledge
d) wisdom

189.

Who was the Lone Ranger's companion?
a) Cato
b) Tonto
c) Geronimo
d) Robin

190.

In 1759, rollerskates were invented in which country?
a) Belgium
b) Germany
c) France
d) England

191.

In which time zone of the U.S. is the State of Wyoming?
a) Mountain Time
b) Pacific Time
c) Central Time
d) Eastern Standard Time

192.

A saying that's been handed down over many years is a
a) proverb
b) a folktale
c) a myth
d) a legend

193.

What name is used to refer to either baby grouse, partridges, or quail?

a) chicks
b) cheepers
c) poult
d) squab

194.

Who wrote the fairy tales The Princess and the Pea and The Emporer's New Clothes?

a) Brothers Grimm
b) Hans Christian Andersen
c) Aesop
d) Charles Perrault

195.

Which is not a country where the Alps—a range of high mountains—exist?

a) Spain
b) Germany
c) Austria
d) Italy

196.

On whose life were many of the incidents that affect the protagonist of this famous novel—*David Copperfield*—based?

a) Charles Dickens
b) Ebenezer Scrooge
c) Mr. Feziwig
d) Bob Cratchit

197.

During which period did Charles Dickens write?
a) Enlightenment
b) Industrial Revolution
c) Age of Reason
d) Age of Technology

198.

Which region of the U.S. did William Faulkner write most about?
a) South
b) East
c) North
d) West

199.

When the mouse ran up it in the rhyme, what time did the clock strike?
a) one
b) two
c) three
d) four

200.

Which range of mountains separates Spain from France?
a) the Alps
b) the Pyrennes
c) the Rocky Mountains
d) the Appalachian Mountains

201.

Which is the birthstone of the month of January?
a) garnet
b) opal
c) pearl
d) onyx

202.

Which historical figure claimed to hear the voices of saints who told her to help restore Charles VII to the throne of France?
a) Joan of Arc
b) Bernadette of Lourdes
c) Mary Baker Eddy
d) none of the above

203.

Who did the Aztec people think Hernan Cortes was when he arrived on horseback and invaded their kindgom?
a) Quetzalcoatl
b) Montezuma
c) a ghost
d) an evil spirit

204.

Where was the frontiersman Davy Crockett killed?
a) Little Big Horn
b) the Alamo
c) the French and Indian War
d) the Revolutionary War

205.

In 1956, who set up the first-ever training school for nurses?
a) Florence Nightingale
b) Elizabeth Cady Stanton
c) Susan B. Anthony
d) Truth Sojourner

206.

Which multi-millionaire retired from business in 1901 and began to donate millions of dollars to worthy causes?
a) Roosevelt
b) Carnegie
c) Vanderbilt
d) Hearst

207.

What order of mammals do whales fall into?
a) Cetacea
b) Carnivora
c) Insectivore
d) Primates

208.

How many time zones are in the lower states of the U.S.?
a) 3
b) 4
c) 5
d) none of the above

209.

What is the name of the day when the sun is nearest to the equator?
a) solstice
b) Halloween
c) equinox
d) Arbor Day

210.

Which leader of the cosmetics industry used her medical knowledge to create a safer line of cosmetics products?
a) Helena Rubenstein
b) Elizabeth Arden
c) Liz Claiborne
d) none of the above

211.

Who founded the Missionaries of Charity?
a) Princess Diana
b) Mother Teresa
c) Mother Cabrini
d) Bernadette of Lourdes

212.

Who played the title role in *The Glenn Miller Story*?
a) Lionel Barrymore
b) Cary Grant
c) James Stewart
d) Kirk Douglas

213.

In 1883, who started a wild west show which starred Annie Oakley and Chief Sitting Bull?
a) Davy Crockett
b) Lewis and Clark
c) Buffalo Bill Cody
d) George Custer

214.

What are Purim, Hanukkah, and Yom Kippur?
a) major holidays of Judaism
b) major holidays of Christianity
c) major holidays of Hinduism
d) none of the above

215.

Which is the birthstone of July?
a) ruby
b) pearl
c) diamond
d) emerald

216.

Where was the wheelbarrow invented?
a) the Americas
b) England
c) China
d) Egypt

217.

Who invented the printing press?
a) Johann Gutenberg
b) Thomas Edison
c) Ben Franklin
d) George Eastman

218.

What order of mammals do humans fall into?
a) Carnivora
b) Insectivora
c) Primates
d) Marsupialia

219.

Who discovered the way to sterilize liquids by heating them to remove bacteria?
a) Louis Pasteur
b) Marie Curie
c) Jonas Salk
d) Albert Einstein

220.

Which scientist won a Nobel Prize in 1904 for his discovery about conditioned reflexes?
a) Ivan Pavlov
b) Albert Einstein
c) Rachel Carson
d) Percival Lowell

221.

Which member of the Rockefeller family joined politics, was governor of New York for fourteen years, and then went on to be U.S. vice president in 1974?
a) John D. Rockefeller, Sr.
b) Nelson Rockefeller
c) John D. Rockefeller, Jr.
d) John D. Rockefeller III

222.

What is a group of crows called?
a) murder
b) flock
c) gaggle
d) yoke

223.

In 1903, who was one of the winners of the Nobel Prize in Physics?
a) Marie Curie
b) Niels Bohr
c) Gabriel Lippmann
d) Albert A. Michelson

224.

Who starred in the 1994 Academy Award-winning movie *Forrest Gump*?
a) Tom Hulce
b) Tom Hanks
c) Tom Ewell
d) Tom Mix

225.

Who founded the religion Buddhism in approximately 525 BC?

a) Siddhartha
b) Mohammed
c) Jesus
d) Gandhi

226.

Which is the birthstone of May?

a) emerald
b) opal
c) onyx
d) pearl

227.

What is a group of bears referred to as?

a) team
b) pod
c) sleuth
d) pack

228.

Where can a stigma, anther, and ovule be found?

a) in a flower
b) in a worm
c) in a meteorite
d) none of the above

229.

Which is the most abundant element on earth?
a) aluminum
b) iron
c) oxygen
d) sodium

230.

Until 1950, what was the most popular girl's name?
a) Helen
b) Anna
c) Mary
d) Linda

231.

Of the names listed, which is the real name of the personality and not a pen name or stage name?
a) Woody Allen
b) Isak Dinesen
c) Mark Twain
d) Charlotte Brontë

232.

Which of these commonly misspelled words is misspelled here?
a) mispell
b) receive
c) accommodate
d) Wednesday

233.

What do Mark McGwire, Tiger Woods, and
Joe DiMaggio have in common?
a) all are from California
b) all are baseball stars
c) all are golf pros
d) none of the above

234.

Who wrote the lyrics to the song "Dream Lover"?
a) Paul Anka
b) Nick Ashford
c) Bobby Darin
d) Paul Williams

235.

In ancient times, who saw the earth's shadow on the
moon during an eclipse and thought the world was a
sphere, not flat as had been believed at the time?
a) Pythagoras
b) Hannibal
c) Genghis Khan
d) Christopher Columbus

236.

Where did the artist Thomas Gainsborough come from?
a) England
b) United States
c) Ireland
d) France

237.

Baby sharks, lions, and bears are commonly called
a) fry
b) cubs
c) pups
d) whelps

238.

Haystack is an impressionist painting done by whom?
a) Monet
b) Picasso
c) Michelangelo
d) Wyeth

239.

In which TV show were June and Ward parents to two sons?
a) *Dobie Gillis*
b) *Leave It to Beaver*
c) *The Donna Reed Show*
d) *Father Knows Best*

240.

Which civilization invented checkers circa 2000 BC?
a) Egyptians
b) Carthaginians
c) Romans
d) Ancient Greeks

241.

In which time zone of the U.S. is the state of Missouri?
a) Mountain Time
b) Central Time
c) Eastern Standard Time
d) Pacific Time

242.

Which women's sporting event held in the U.S. in 1999 drew a record crowd of over 90,000?
a) the World Cup Women's Title Game
b) the U.S. Open
c) the Super Bowl
d) the World Series

243.

What is the state motto of New York?
a) Excelsior!
b) Live Free or Die!
c) Go East!
d) I Love New York

244.

Who was named the Most Valuable Player for the Broncos during the Super Bowl XXXIII game?
a) Joe Namath
b) John Elway
c) Phil Simms
d) none of the above

245.

In game five of the 1999 NBA finals, which team lost to the San Antonio Spurs?
a) New York Knicks
b) Boston Celtics
c) Los Angeles Lakers
d) Detroit Pistons

246.

Where can the U.S. Capitol Building, the Lincoln Memorial, and the White House be seen?
a) on the back side of U.S. currency
b) Washington, D.C.
c) a map
d) all of the above

247.

Who or what was the popular derby hat named after?
a) the 12th Earl of Derby
b) headgear worn by Kentucky Derby jockeys
c) a hat worn by soapbox car racers
d) none of the above

248.

Where is the Kennedy Space Center located?
a) New York
b) Massachusetts
c) Florida
d) California

249.

Which of these musical pieces didn't George Gershwin compose?
a) *Rhapsody in Blue*
b) *An American in Paris*
c) *Porgy and Bess*
d) *Appalachian Spring*

250.

Where are these three great composers from: Schubert, Strauss and Mozart?
a) Germany
b) Austria
c) Spain
d) France

251.

Where is the Arizona Memorial located?
a) Pearl Harbor
b) San Francisco Bay
c) Lake Superior
d) the Gulf of Mexico

252.

Which word means to inform?
a) apprise
b) appraise
c) applaud
d) appease

253.

Which team is considered to be the Team of the Century for winning the 1999 World Series and the previous World Series as well?
a) New York Yankees
b) Atlanta Braves
c) Baltimore Orioles
d) St. Louis Cardinals

254.

Which is not an Elvis Presley film?
a) *Love Me Tender*
b) *Jailhouse Rock*
c) *G. I. Blues*
d) *A Hard Day's Night*

255.

What does cum laude mean?
a) with praise
b) with care
c) with pride
d) with knowledge

256.

What is one of the best-known works of the French composer Maurice Ravel, which was featured in the movie *10* starring Bo Derek and Dudley Moore?
a) *Bolero*
b) *Parade*
c) *Samson et Dalila*
d) *Rhapsodie espagnole*

257.

In the proverb, what do actions speak louder than?
a) pictures
b) words
c) sportscasters
d) none of the above

258.

Which of these American composers received the 1945 Pulitzer Prize?
A) Aaron Copland
b) Leonard Bernstein
c) George Gershwin
d) Walter Piston

259.

Which did Mozart compose first?
a) *Le Nozze di Figaro*
b) *Don Giovanni*
c) *The Magic Flute*
d) *Requiem*

260.

To keep the doctor away, you should have one of these every day
a) a vitamin
b) an apple
c) a bath
d) a haircut

261.

Which is an animated movie starring the Beatles?
a) *A Hard Day's Night*
b) *Yellow Submarine*
c) *The Long and Winding Road*
d) *I Want to Hold Your Hand*

262.

How was the torch used at the Olympic Games first lit?
a) by the sun's rays at Olympia in Greece
b) match
c) Zippo lighter
d) none of the above

263.

Who holds the record for most NHL goals in one season for 1981-1982?
a) Wayne Gretzky
b) Brett Hull
c) Mario Lemieux
d) Mike Bossy

264.

Who was only the fourth player in history to rush for over 2000 yards in a season?
a) Terrell Davis
b) Joe Namath
c) Phil Simms
d) Doug Flutie

265.

Which is the flower of September?
a) morning glory
b) rose
c) chrysanthemum
d) lily

266.

What does biennial mean?
a) every two years
b) every two days
c) every two months
d) every two decades

267.

What is the equivalent of 1,000,000 in Roman numerals?
a) C
b) $\overline{M}$
c) L
d) D

268.

Where were Johann S. Bach, Ludwig van Beethoven, and Johannes Brahms from?
a) Germany
b) Austria
c) France
d) Spain

269.

Who holds the record for most NHL goals in one season for 1970-71?
a) Phil Esposito
b) Guy Lafleur
c) Wayne Gretzky
d) Mario Lemieux

270.

Which city is the setting for *The Drew Carey Show?*
a) Atlanta
b) Cleveland
c) Chicago
d) Dallas

271.

What does the word verbatim mean?
a) word for word
b) danger
c) exit
d) none of the above

272.

In 1952, who was arrested for voting?
a) Susan B. Anthony
b) Rosa Parks
c) Julia Ward Howe
d) Elizabeth Cady Stanton

273.

Which was written by F. Scott Fitzgerald in 1925?
a) *The Beautiful and Damned*
b) *The Great Gatsby*
c) *The Last Tycoon*
d) none of the above

274.

What was the name of the film of Carl Bernstein and Bob Woodward's discovery of the Watergate break-in?
a) *All the President's Men*
b) *Manchurian Candidate*
c) *A Good Man is Hard to Find*
d) *Roman Holiday*

275.

What is the nickname of Missouri?
a) Show Me State
b) Aloha State
c) Sunshine State
d) Garden State

276.

What do Cochise, Geronimo, and Barry Goldwater have in common?
a) all are famous Arizonans
b) all are Aries
c) all are politicians
d) all succeeded at a young age

277.

Who did the New York Yankees beat to win the 1999 World Series?
a) Boston Red Sox
b) Baltimore Orioles
c) Atlanta Braves
d) St. Louis Cardinals

278.

Of these famous Italian composers, which lived to see the 20th Century?
a) Bellini
b) Puccini
c) Rossini
d) Vivaldi

279.

What opera of Puccini was completed posthumously by Franco Alfano?
a) *Turandot*
b) *Le Bohème*
c) *Tosca*
d) *Madame Butterfly*

280.

Which Michael Jackson album featured a voice over by Vincent Price?
a) Thriller
b) Bad
c) Dangerous
d) Off the Wall

281.

A leopard cannot
a) outrun a fox
b) change his tune
c) change his spots
d) change his mind

282.

In 1754
a) the Boston Tea party took place
b) the French and Indian War began
c) George Washington was named commander-in-chief
d) the Bill of Rights went into effect

283.

In 1851, who wrote the acclaimed novel *Moby Dick*?
a) Edgar Allan Poe
b) Herman Melville
c) Walt Whitman
d) Henry David Thoreau

284.

Which state is known as the Sunshine State?
a) Arizona
b) Kentucky
c) Florida
d) Georgia

285.

What is the name of the progressive, degenerative disease of the brain in which brain cells die and are not replaced?
a) dementia
b) Alzheimer's Disease
c) Parkinson's Disease
d) Legionnaire's Disease

286.

What is the name of the chronic disease when the body doesn't produce enough of or properly use insulin?
a) psoriosis
b) diabetes
c) cancer
d) heart disease

287.

Which two operas are Rossini known for?
a) *William Tell*
b) *The Barber of Seville*
c) *Swan Lake*
d) *The Sleeping Beauty*

288.

Rigoletto, Traviata, and *Otello* are operas composed by
a) Giuseppe Verdi
b) Giacomo Puccini
c) Antono Vivaldi
d) none of the above

289.

In the *Music Man*, what did the character played by Robert Preston make believe he was?

a) a music professor
b) a shoe salesman
c) a doctor
d) a pool player

290.

What is the equivalent of 5000 in Roman numerals?

a) $\overline{V}$
b) X
c) D
d) M

291.

The Pittsburgh Steelers have won two consecutive Super Bowl games twice; which were the first consecutive wins?

a) IX and X
b) I and II
c) XXX and XXXI
d) none of the above

292.

Which environmental crisis has to do with the earth getting warmer?

a) ozone hole
b) acid rain
c) greenhouse effect
d) none of the above

293.

Which phenomenon is having a harmful environmental effect on the world's forests?
a) ozone hole
b) acid rain
c) greenhouse effect
d) aurora borealis

294.

Where is it believed that Leif Erikson explored?
a) North America
b) India
c) Southeast Asia
d) Antarctica

295.

What do sloths, hairy anteaters, and armadillos have in common?
a) all are toothless mammals
b) all are carnivores
c) all are marsupials
d) all fly

296.

If you blow hot and cold it means you
a) are waiting for a storm
b) change your mind constantly
c) have the flu
d) none of the above

297.

What do vertebrates have that invertebrates don't have?
a) backbone
b) fingernails
c) exoskeleton
d) two legs

298.

Which are three epochs of the Mesozoic Era?
a) Creteaceous
b) Jurassic
c) Triassic
d) Paleocene

299.

Harriet Beecher Stowe was the author of which book published in 1852?
a) *Uncle Tom's Cabin*
b) *The Pit and the Pendulum*
c) *The Secret Garden*
d) *The Underground Railroad*

300.

What does the term allegro mean in music?
a) play music quickly
b) play music with passion
c) play music slowly
d) stop playing

301.

Which is not an American choreographer?
a) Alvin Ailey
b) Agnes DeMille
c) Martha Graham
d) Alicia Alonso

302.

In which 1977 film did Mikhail Baryshnikov co-star with Gregory Hines?
a) *The Turning Point*
b) *Flashdance*
c) *An American in Paris*
d) *Staying Alive*

303.

Winslow Homer, one of the most prominent 19th-century American painters, is famous for which work of art?
a) *Winter*
b) *Toilers of the Sea*
c) *The Hurricane*
d) none of the above

304.

Who was the first African-American U.S. Supreme Court Justice?
a) Thurgood Marshall
b) William Rehnquist
c) Clarence Thomas
d) Harlan Stone

305.

Which event happened in 1773?
a) the BostonTea Party
b) the signing of the Constitution
c) Paul Revere's Ride
d) Lincoln's assassination

306.

Where does the saying, "Money is the root of all evil," come from?
a) *Farmer's Almanac*
b) the Bible
c) *Book of Quotations*
d) none of the above

307.

As the crow flies means?
a) how high off the ground a bird flies
b) the most direct route
c) night has come
d) north by northwest

308.

In computer terms, hacker means?
a) someone with a cough
b) someone with a temper
c) a novice
d) a mischief maker

309.

What is the nickname of Hawaii?
a) Aloha State
b) Empire State
c) Pineapple State
d) Sunshine State

310.

Who portrayed Edward Rochester in the feature film
Jane Eyre?
a) Joseph Cotten
b) Orson Welles
c) George C. Scott
d) Lawrence Olivier

311.

Which American painter was born in Russia?
a) Norman Rockwell
b) Maxfield Parrish
c) Howard Pyle
d) Mark Rothko

312.

Which movement in art did Arshile Gorky influence?
a) Impressionism
b) Cubism
c) Abstract Expressionism
d) Pointillism

313.

In 1902, who discovered radium?
a) Pierre and Marie Curie
b) Albert Einstein
c) Fritz Haber
d) Georges Claude

314.

Which is a famous American composer of the 20th century?
a) Albin Berg
b) Thomas Morly
c) Paul Dukas
d) Leonard Bernstein

315.

What is worth a thousand words?
a) a picture
b) a single thought
c) one kind word
d) a great idea

316.

Which were the second two consecutive Super Bowl games won by the Pittsburgh Steelers?
a) VI and VII
b) XI and XII
c) XIII and XIV
d) IX and X

317.

Who was the winning coach both times when the
Pittsburgh Steelers won each of their two consecutive
Super Bowl games?
a) Chuck Noll
b) Bill Austin
c) Joe Bach
d) Raymond Parker

318.

In 1905, which scientific discovery did Albert
Einstein make?
a) theory of relativity
b) quantum theory
c) Doppler principle
d) quantum mechanics

319.

Who won the XXIII and XXIV Super Bowl games?
a) Green Bay Packers
b) San Francisco 49ers
c) Dallas Cowboys
d) Denver Broncos

320.

What is the mother of invention?
a) creativity
b) necessity
c) desperation
d) none of the above

321.

If you receive an item in the mail that you didn't order, you
a) must return it
b) must pay for it
c) can keep it free of charge
d) none of the above

322.

Where did artist Hieronymous Bosch come from?
a) Holland
b) France
c) Germany
d) Austria

323.

Paul Cezanne was a famous Impressionist from which country?
a) France
b) Holland
c) Canada
d) Austria

324.

Where does someone wishing to become a citizen of the U.S. apply?
a) Immigration and Naturalization Service
b) Dept. of Interior
c) Dept. of Defense
d) Dept. of Commerce

325.

What is the chief mandate of Interpol?

a) promote assistance among worldwide police authorities

b) promote worldwide communication

c) promote use of the Internet

d) promote public opinion polling

326.

What does Eureka! mean?

a) you've found something you've been looking for

b) something smells

c) it's time to vacuum

d) none of the above

327.

Which movie did Charles Laughton direct?

a) *The Canterbury Ghost*

b) *The Night of the Hunter*

c) *Private Life of Henry VIII*

d) *The Big Clock*

328.

In 1941, which movie won the Academy Award for Best Picture?

a) *The Blue Angel*

b) *How Green Was My Valley*

c) *It's a Wonderful Life*

d) *The Lion in Winter*

329.

Which is not a letter from the Hebrew alphabet?
a) iota
b) sin
c) tav
d) mem

330.

Which is a word, phrase, sentence, or numeral that spells the same way forward and backward called?
a) palindrome
b) hippodrome
c) homophone
d) digraph

331.

What is truth stranger than?
a) non-fiction
b) science fiction
c) fiction
d) history

332.

Which civilization was the first to write and amass literature?
a) Sumerians
b) Babylonians
c) Egyptians
d) Assyrians

333.

Which movie musical features the George Gershwin song "Love is Here to Stay"?
a) *Oklahoma*
b) *An American in Paris*
c) *Carousel*
d) *West Side Story*

334.

In the Middle Ages, which was the popular form of literature?
a) novel
b) sonnet
c) short story
d) epic poem

335.

In Internet lingo, what does F2F stand for?
a) face to face
b) friend to friend
c) a connectivity issue
d) none of the above

336.

In computer terms, application means
a) a program designed for a specific task
b) a file
c) a unit of data
d) a collection of information

337.

When you're in hot water it means
a) you're taking a bath
b) you're in trouble for something
c) you're in a sauna
d) you're in a spa

338.

In which decade did *Annie Hall*, *The Deer Hunter*, and *Rocky* win Best Picture of the Year awards?
a) 1960s
b) 1970s
c) 1980s
d) none of the above

339.

Who played the female lead in *Shakespeare in Love*, which won the 1998 Academy Award for Best Picture of the Year?
a) Gwyneth Paltrow
b) Susan Sarandon
c) Sarah Jessica Parker
d) Nicole Kidman

340.

Which team lost four consecutive Super Bowl games, 1991-1994?
a) Washington Redskins
b) Oakland Raiders
c) Green Bay Packers
d) Buffalo Bills

341.

If you make ends meet, you
a) tied the ends of a string together
b) are managing the best you can with the resources at hand
c) drew a circle
d) did something justified

342.

In 1777, when the U.S. flag was designed, what was the significance of the field of blue with 13 stars?
a) a new constellation
b) a new era
c) independence
d) good luck

343.

Where is Badlands National Park?
a) South Dakota
b) New Orleans
c) Kentucky
d) Virginia

344.

Who is floating face down in a swimming pool in the opening scene of the movie *Sunset Boulevard*?
a) James Mason
b) Cary Grant
c) William Holden
d) Burt Lancaster

345.

Touché is a word associated with
a) football
b) soccer
c) fencing
d) aerobics

346.

A person who is not what he seems is known as
a) A Catcher in the Rye
b) a wolf in sheep's clothing
c) an entrepreneur
d) a salesman

347.

When you break the ice, you
a) use a sledgehammer
b) become comfortable in a situation
c) get ice cubes
d) none of the above

348.

Which painting is Edgar Degas known for?
a) *Tiger Attacking a Horse*
b) *Water Lilies*
c) *The File Player*
d) *Woman with Chrysanthemums*

349.

Which work of art is an example of Claude Monet's Impressionism?
a) *Water Lilies*
b) *Starry Night*
c) *Resurrection*
d) *Sugaring-off*

350.

Who wrote the song "One Last Bell to Answer" with Hal David?
a) Paul Anka
b) Burt Bacharach
c) Paul Williams
d) Nick Ashford

351.

What is A.M. an abbreviation for?
a) after meals
b) ante mezzo
c) before noon
d) in the morning

352.

Does someone who has a bee in his bonnet
a) risk getting stung
b) complain constantly about the same thing
c) like to wear hats
d) run a bee farm

353.

If you get forty winks does it mean you have
a) an eye impairment
b) taken a nap or slept
c) an admirer
d) none of the above

354.

Merci is the French word for
a) mercy
b) thank you
c) good day
d) waiter

355.

If you plan on attending a party, you'd better return one of these
a) WASP
b) RSVP
c) SASE
d) FYI

356.

Which historical period included these major styles of art: Byzantine, Romanesque, and Gothic?
a) the Middle Ages
b) the Renaissance
c) the Modern Age
d) Classicism

357.

Having cold feet means
a) you've changed your mind
b) forgot to put your socks on
c) fell through the ice
d) none of the above

358.

The Modern Era of art, from 1776 to the present, included all but which?
a) Romanticism
b) Impressionism
c) Cubism
d) Classicism

359.

Which is the flower of June?
a) zinnia
b) daisy
c) rose
d) tulip

360.

In which movie did Keanu Reeves portray an undercover police officer posing as a surfer?
a) *Point Break*
b) *Matrix*
c) *Speed*
d) *Commando*

361.

In 1762, who invented the sandwich?
a) the 4th Earl of Sandwich
b) Jonas Salk
c) Carl Sandburg
d) John Singer Sargent

362.

Where is the United Nations — established in 1945 — headquartered?
a) New York, N.Y.
b) Paris, France
c) London, England
d) Brussels, Belgium

363.

In classical mythology, who was the brother of Zeus?
a) Poseidon
b) Kronos
c) Hermes
d) Uranus

364.

Which three are sons of Zeus?
a) Apollo
b) Ares
c) Dionysus
d) Hades

365.

Which is not an oxymoron?
a) good grief
b) soft rock
c) easy as pie
d) alone together

366.

What does the Greek prefix cardio- mean?
a) joint
b) throat
c) blood
d) heart

367.

Vice versa is Latin for
a) upside down
b) inside out
c) the other way around
d) helter skelter

368.

The land of Canaan was the Promised Land God gave to
a) Adam and Eve
b) Abraham and his descendants
c) Pharaoh
d) Noah

369.

What is the name of the tower built by the descendants of Noah?
a) Babel
b) Sears Tower
c) Coit Tower
d) Tower of London

370.

What are the internationally recognized treaties that govern the protection of civilians, the treatment of prisoners, and the caring of the wounded and sick during time of war called?
a) Geneva Convention
b) NATO
c) Brussels Pact
d) Peace of Prussia

371.

In 1784, who invented the bifocal lens?
a) Ben Franklin
b) Thomas Jefferson
c) Eli Whitney
d) none of the above

372.

What is the mandate of the United Nations?
a) promote justice for all
b) maintain world peace and security
c) lobby for human rights
d) represent all nations

373.

What was the name of the 1876 world's fair held in Philadelphia, Pennsylvania?

a) Crystal Palace Exposition
b) Centennial Exposition
c) Universal Exposition
d) Century 21 Exposition

374.

In 1900, what did Thomas Edison invent?

a) telegraph
b) telephone
c) microwave
d) alkaline battery

375.

In 1965, which company invented the word processor?

a) Sony
b) IBM
c) General Electric
d) Westinghouse

376.

Which 1957 musical did Leonard Bernstein compose, which was later made into a motion picture starring Natalie Wood?

a) *West Side Story*
b) *Carousel*
c) *State Fair*
d) *The Pirates of Penzance*

377.

Who was the great Greek warrior of the Trojan War whose mother bathed him in a magical river as a baby to make him immortal?
a) Perseus
b) Adonis
c) Achilles
d) Prometheus

378.

Aphrodite is known as the goddess of
a) war
b) love
c) fertility
d) prosperity

379.

What was the mythological race of strong, fearless warrior women called?
a) Rockettes
b) Amazons
c) DAR
d) goddesses

380.

Who was the 16th vice president of the U.S. and served with Abraham Lincoln?
a) Andrew Johnson
b) John Adams
c) George Washington
d) Martin van Buren

381.

Which is the nickname for bowling?

a) tenpins
b) slam 'em
c) knock down
d) strike

382.

Which is the object of the game football?

a) to move the ball down the field and across the goal line into the opponent's end zone
b) to knock down wooden pins with a ball
c) to score points by hitting the ball so your opponent can't return it
d) to score more runs than the opposing team

383.

What part of Achilles' — the great Greek warrior of the Trojan Wars — body was susceptible to danger?

a) his heel
b) his elbow
c) his wrist
d) his toe

384.

Which of these events happened in 1716?

a) the first labor organization in the U.S. was founded
b) the first circulating library opened in Philadelphia
c) the first theater opened in the colonies in Williamsburg, Virginia
d) the first Indian reservation was established

385.

The Amazon River is named for a mythological race of warrior women.
a) true
b) false

386.

On which U.S. TV show did the Beatles first appear?
a) *Steve Allen Show*
b) *Ed Sullivan Show*
c) *Mike Douglas Show*
d) *Tonight Show*

387.

What is the Roman name of the Greek goddess Aphrodite?
a) Claris
b) Venus
c) Hera
d) Athena

388.

What happened in 1789?
a) George Washington was elected to be the first president
b) the Bill of Rights went into effect
c) the Boston Tea Party
d) the Sugar Tax was levied

389.

Which TV program began with the words "These are the voyages of the starship Enterprise..."?

a) *Lost in Space*
b) *Star Trek*
c) *My Favorite Martian*
d) *The Avenger*

390.

Where was the home of King Arthur's court?

a) Valhalla
b) Shangri-la
c) Camelot
d) Styxx

391.

When did Henry David Thoreau's *Walden* first get published?

a) 1754
b) 1854
c) 1954
d) none of the above

392.

In 1992, who was the Women's Wimbledon Champion?

a) Steffi Graf
b) Gabriela Sabatini
c) Monica Seles
d) Martina Hingis

393.

The name Adonis is associated with
a) beauty
b) wealth
c) success
d) wisdom

394.

Where is the world's tallest stalagmite?
a) Czech Republic
b) France
c) Africa
d) United States

395.

Who is the father of Apollo?
a) Poseidon
b) Thor
c) Zeus
d) Hermes

396.

In the Greek language, what does naut mean?
a) sailor
b) doctor
c) lawyer
d) writer

397.

Which is one of the most often performed songs?

a) Auld Lang Syne

b) Yankee Doodle Dandy

c) Born Free

d) This Land is Your Land

398.

What is fusion-jazz a combination of?

a) rock and jazz

b) country and hip hop

c) rap and jazz

d) none of the above

399.

In 1976, who was the Women's Wimbledon Champion?

a) Billie Jean King

b) Tracy Austin

c) Chris Evert

d) Margaret Smith Court

400.

What incredible feat did King Arthur accomplish as a boy?

a) he took the sword Excalibur out of a stone

b) he killed the Cyclops

c) he swam the English Channel

d) he climbed Mount Everest

401.

What did Jason and the Argonauts go in search of?
a) the Holy Grail
b) the Golden Fleece
c) a Golden Parachute
d) the Cyclops

402.

According to mythology, which bird became endowed with Argus' eyes?
a) the peacock
b) the flamingo
c) the eagle
d) the dove

403.

Diana, the goddess of the hunt, is also known as
a) Artemis
b) Pandora
c) Hera
d) Athena

404.

In 1860, which mail service traveled between Sacramento, California, and St. Joseph, Missouri?
a) the Pony Express
b) United Parcel Service
c) Federal Express
d) DHL

405.

Before reaching the pinnacle of fame as a movie star, which actor first co-starred in a TV western?
a) George Peppard
b) Bruce Willlis
c) Clint Eastwood
d) James Arness

406.

What does the ozone do for earth?
a) protects it from the sun's rays
b) keeps it in orbit around the sun
c) helps it rotate daily
d) none of the above

407.

In the 1300s, where did Marco Polo's explorations take him?
a) Far East and India
b) North America
c) Nova Scotia
d) South Pacific

408.

From which time period does the legend of King Arthur come?
a) Dark Ages
b) Industrial Age
c) Middle Ages
d) Iron Age

409.

Which is an oxymoron?
a) pretty ugly
b) silly sally
c) dressed to kill
d) under the gun

410.

What are kaf, vav, and he?
a) endangered species
b) desserts
c) letters from the Hebrew alphabet
d) none of the above

411.

Word prefixes can come from Greek or Latin origins. What does the Greek prefix encephal- mean?
a) brain
b) heart
c) gut
d) head

412.

Who was Morgan le Fay?
a) an enchantress
b) a lounge singer
b) a fashion designer
d) a financier

413.

In which show was Peter Graves greeted with the message "Good morning, Mr. Phelps..."?
a) *Hawaii Five-0*
b) *Mission Impossible*
c) *Get Smart*
d) none of the above

414.

At the end of King Arthur's life, where does legend say he went?
a) Avalon
b) Camelot
c) Babylon
d) Club Med

415.

In 1865, where did General Robert E. Lee surrender to General Ulysses S. Grant?
a) Appomattox Court House, Virginia
b) Gettysburg, Pennsylvania
c) Atlanta, Georgia
d) Charleston, South Carolina

416.

Where in New York was the first F.W. Woolworth five and dime store opened?
a) Buffalo
b) Utica
c) Albany
d) New York City

417.

What happened on August 15, 1914?
a) World War II ended
b) stock market crash
c) Panama Canal opened
d) none of the above

418.

What is the study of the effect on human behavior of the planets, moon, stars, and sun called?
a) astronomy
b) astrology
c) trigonometry
d) telepathy

419.

If warmer temperatures due to the greenhouse effect occur, what do scientists believe will happen?
a) low-lying cities would flood
b) continents would eventually be covered with ice
c) the earth would rotate faster
d) none of the above

420.

Which of the Knights of the Round Table fell in love with Queen Guinevere?
a) Sir Galahad
b) Sir Gawain
c) Sir Lancelot
d) Sir Percival

421.

In the 1700s, who explored the South Pacific?
a) Sir Richard Burton
b) James Cook
c) Robert Scott
d) Roald Amundsen

422.

Which singer had the "wedding bell blues"?
a) Barbra Streisand
b) Marilyn McCoo
c) Grace Slick
d) Mama Cass

423.

Who was born from the head of Zeus?
a) Athena
b) Perseus
c) Hera
d) Cassiopeia

424.

What mythological god or goddess was the city Athens named for?
a) Artemis
b) Athena
c) Ares
d) Argus

425.

Which gang did Butch Cassidy lead in the movie *Butch Cassidy and the Sundance Kid*?
a) Our Gang
b) Eastside Kids
c) the Hole in the Wall Gang
d) Mousketeers

426.

Which is not an oxymoron?
a) sweet sorrow
b) never the twain shall meet
c) exact estimate
d) working vacation

427.

What does the Greek prefix hydro- mean?
a) water
b) above
c) sleep
d) under

428.

Which Trojan War hero did the goddess Athena help to guide home?
a) Paris
b) Menelaus
c) Odysseus
d) Perseus

429.

Under which ocean is the mythical island of Atlantis supposedly lost beneath?
a) Pacific Ocean
b) Indian Ocean
c) Arctic Ocean
d) Atlantic Ocean

430.

Which constellation can be seen in the northern hemisphere?
a) Aquarius
b) Scorpio
c) Pegasus
d) Libra

431.

Which continent is west of Madagascar?
a) Australia
b) Africa
c) Asia
d) none of the above

432.

Which country won the War of 1812?
a) Britain
b) United States
c) France
d) Spain

433.

Who did Natalie Wood portray in the film *West Side Story?*
a) Anita
b) Maria
c) Ana
d) Luisa

434.

Which building in the U.S. is the tallest?
a) World Trade Center
b) Sears Tower
c) Chrysler Building
d) Empire State Building

435.

Which is the largest desert in the world?
a) Australian
b) Arabian
c) Sahara
d) Gobi

436.

Which was the first major international TV broadcast?
a) the wedding of Diana Spencer to Prince Charles
b) the first walk on the moon
c) the coronation of Queen Elizabeth II
d) none of the above

437.

Where did ballet, as we know it today, begin?

a) Italy
b) France
c) Austria
d) Germany

438.

When do a birdie, an eagle, and a fairway go together?

a) when you're birdwatching
b) when you're playing golf
c) when you're playing badminton
d) in extreme sports

439.

Which famous American novel begins, "Call me, Ishmael"?

a) *The Old Man and the Sea*
b) *Moby Dick*
c) *The Book of Daniel*
d) *The Golden Bowl*

440.

Who directed the movie *Gone with the Wind*?

a) Alfred Hitchcock
b) Victor Fleming
c) Frank Capra
d) John Ford

441.

Who said "The greatest remedy for anger is delay"?
a) Shakespeare
b) Seneca
c) Plato
d) Confucius

442.

Which sea surrounds the eastern side of the United Kingdom?
a) Black Sea
b) North Sea
c) Baltic Sea
d) Adriatic Sea

443.

Which bird can hover like a helicopter?
a) a finch
b) a swallow
c) a hummingbird
d) a parakeet

444.

Which state is the Empire State of the South?
a) Tennessee
b) Georgia
c) Alabama
d) South Carolina

445.

Who created the character Sherlock Holmes?
a) H.G. Wells
b) Sir Arthur Conan Doyle
c) Rudyard Kipling
d) Rider Haggard

446.

Contrary to the beliefs of the time, what did Hippocrates espouse?
a) illness was not caused by evil spirits
b) health was all in the mind
c) a happy person is a healthy person
d) an apple a day keeps the doctor away

447.

How did Galileo do his research on the physics of movement?
a) he dropped an apple from a tree to the ground
b) he dropped objects from the Leaning Tower of Pisa
c) he read the shadow of the sun
d) he used a telescope

448.

Who is the Greek goddess of vengeance?
a) Persephone
b) Hades
c) Nemesis
d) Eris

449.

Who said "Knowledge is power"?
a) Aristotle
b) Francis Bacon
c) Mark Twain
d) Ben Franklin

450.

Which is an oxymoron?
a) asleep on your feet
b) slow as molasses
c) genuine imitation
d) running scared

451.

When were the *Tales of King Arthur, Beowulf,* and the *Canterbury Tales* written?
a) Renaissance
b) Middle Ages
c) Age of Reason
d) Realism

452.

When was the first transcontinental telephone call completed?
a) 1915
b) 1945
c) 1950
d) none of the above

453.

Quantum, molecular, and atomic are specialties of the study of which science?
a) chemistry
b) biology
c) physics
d) anatomy

454.

What did Mitzi Gaynor wash right out of her hair in the popular song from the musical movie version of *South Pacific*?
a) shampoo
b) that man
c) gum
d) confetti

455.

What feat did Alexander Graham Bell and Thomas Watson achieve in 1915?
a) they completed the first transcontinental telephone call
b) they formed the first telephone company
c) they developed an inexpensive telephone device
d) they invented the touchtone telephone

456.

Who is often referred to as "the once and future king"?
a) Old King Cole
b) King Arthur
c) King Tut
d) Nat King Cole

457.

Who wrote *The Sun Also Rises*, which was published in 1926?
a) Pearl Buck
b) Ernest Hemingway
c) Eugene O'Neill
d) none of the above

458.

Who directed *The Wizard of Oz*?
a) Cecil B. DeMille
b) Victor Fleming
c) Orson Welles
d) Vincente Minnelli

459.

During which period of literature were *Hamlet*, *Don Quixote*, and the *Book of Songs* written?
a) Renaissance
b) Modern Age
c) Classicism
d) Ancient Times

460.

In classical mythology, who supports the earth and sky on his shoulders?
a) Cyclops
b) Atlas
c) Griffin
d) Hercules

461.

In which fairy tale does a beautiful, gentle woman come to love and be loved by a hideous beast?

a) Rapunzel

b) Beauty and the Beast

c) The Princess and the Pea

d) The Sleeping Beauty

462.

In computer terms, boot means

a) kick your computer

b) change a tire

c) start up your computer

d) quit all applications

463.

In computer terms, crash mean

a) spend the night

b) lose control

c) short circuit

d) failure of a program or a disk

464.

What does the Latin prefix retro- mean?

a) backward

b) upside down

c) forward

d) horizontally

465.

Which was not written during the Age of Reason?
a) *Candide*
b) *Paradise Lost*
c) *Romeo and Juliet*
d) *Gulliver's Travels*

466.

In computer terms, CD-ROM means
a) compact disk read-only memory
b) a communications network
c) a disk drive
d) a compact disk player

467.

In which time zone of the U.S. is the state of Nevada?
a) Central Time
b) Pacific Time
c) Eastern Standard Time
d) Mountain Time

468.

Social dances, those performed by couples, including the tango, cha-cha, and waltz, are known as
a) country dances
b) folk dances
c) square dances
d) ballroom dances

469.

Where did the dance the Conga originate?
a) England
b) Haiti
c) Spain
d) Africa-Cuba

470.

Which singing duo had a popular TV variety show in the 1970s?
a) Jan and Dean
b) Sonny and Cher
c) Lewis and Martin
d) Simon and Garfunkle

471.

In 1878, who invented the phonograph?
a) Thomas Edison
b) Alexander Graham Bell
c) Edwin Hubble
d) none of the above

472.

In the fairy tale Bluebeard, how many of his wives failed Bluebeard's test of obedience and paid with their lives?
a) 5
b) 6
c) 7
d) 8

473.

Which name can be described as: a legendary blue ox, a famous baseball player, and a pig?
a) Burt
b) Charlotte
c) Babe
d) Arnold

474.

Where did the legendary lumberjack Paul Bunyan roam?
a) Swiss Alps
b) Northern U.S. and Canada
c) Alaska
d) Nova Scotia

475.

Who won the Stanley Cup four consecutive seasons from 1979-83?
a) New York Islanders
b) Pittsburgh Penguins
c) Montreal Canadiens
d) Edmonton Oilers

476.

What was the name of the aircraft flown by Charles Lindbergh from to Paris in 1926?
a) the Spirit of St. Augustus
b) the Spirit of St. Charles
c) the Spirit of St. Louis
d) the Spirit of St. Cloud

477.

Who wrote the novel *The Good Earth,* which was published in 1931?
a) Pearl Buck
b) Edith Wharton
c) Virginia Wolf
d) Katherine Mansfield

478.

What do King Arthur and John F. Kennedy have in common?
a) both reigned in "Camelot"
b) both were kings
c) both are on postage stamps
d) none of the above

479.

Which is considered to be the greatest work of Ludwig van Beethoven?
a) Ninth Symphony
b) Fidelio
c) 6th Symphony
d) none

480.

Which of these Russian composers was also a conductor?
a) Stravinsky
b) Tchaikovsky
c) Borodin
d) Rachmaninoff

481.

What is the name of some of the Hindu sacred books?
a) Bhagavad Gita
b) Old Testament
c) Torah
d) Koran

482.

What is the biggest mammal that ever lived?
a) African elephant
b) blue whale
c) gray whale
d) none of the above

483.

Which composer is best known for the opera *Carmen*,
composed in 1875?
a) Hector Belioz
b) Paul Dukas
c) Georges Bizet
d) Claude Debussy

484.

On TV's *Happy Days*, what role did Henry Winkler play?
a) the Fonz
b) Richie Cunningham
c) Ralph Malph
d) Arnold

485.

What is Nirvana?
a) the state of total peace
b) a pain killer
c) a prescription drug
d) none of the above

486.

Which English playwright is known for the play
The Taming of the Shrew?
a) Marlowe
b) Shakespeare
c) Webster
d) Coward

487.

Which is not a work of playwright William Shakespeare?
a) *Hamlet*
b) *Romeo and Juliet*
c) *Tamburlaine*
d) *As You Like It*

488.

Which is not a 19th-century dramatist?
a) Victor Hugo
b) Henrik Ibsen
c) Harold Pinter
d) Oscar Wilde

489.

Who wrote *Don Quixote?*
a) Mario Puzo
b) Miguel de Cervantes
c) Franz Kafka
d) Arthur Miller

490.

Who is the hero of a famous epic from Spain?
a) El Al
b) Eloise
c) El Cid
d) El Niño

491.

Who was Confucius?
a) a Chinese philosopher
b) the founder of ethical principles
c) a philosopher whose teachings are well known as short sayings
d) all of the above

492.

What do gray, blue, white, and pilot refer to?
a) types of whales
b) kinds of heat
c) kinds of lightning
d) military uniforms

493.

Which German composer had 20 children, 10 of whom survived?

a) Ludwig van Beethoven
c) Johannes Brahms
c) Johann S. Bach
d) Richard Wagner

494.

Which Russian composer's work, *Rite of Spring*, is featured in the Walt Disney classic animated film *Fantasia*?

a) Igor Stravinsky
b) Rachmaninoff
c) Borodin
d) Tchaikovsky

495.

What does the term adagio mean when music is performed?

a) play music slowly
b) play music quickly
c) play music with animation
d) play music with passion

496.

Which classic children's book was not written by E.B. White?

a) *Stuart Little*
b) *Charlotte's Web*
c) *Where The Wild Things Are*
d) *The Trumpet of the Swan*

497.

Where was gunpowder invented?
a) China
b) Germany
c) France
d) United States

498.

When did the White House first become the official home of the U.S. presidents?
a) 1776
b) 1800
c) 1849
d) 1864

499.

Who won the Stanley Cup five consecutive seasóns from 1955-60?
a) Montreal Canadiens
b) Chicago Black Hawks
c) Boston Bruins
d) Toronto Maple Leafs

500.

Whose life story did James Cagney play in the film *Yankee Doodle Dandy?*
a) Ira Gershwin
b) George M. Cohan
c) Aaron Copland
d) Irving Berlin

501.

Which alphabet is the Russian language written in?
a) Latin
b) Hieroglyphs
c) Cyrillic
d) Arabic

502.

Who was the star of the 1992 Academy Award-winning movie *Unforgiven*?
a) Tom Hanks
b) Jack Nicholson
c) Clint Eastwood
d) Tom Cruise

503.

Which is not a 20th-century playwright?
a) Eugene O'Neill
b) Samuel Beckett
c) Oscar Wilde
d) Anton Chekov

504.

Which is not a famous name in architecture?
a) Charles Bulfinch
b) Le Corbusier
c) Seneca
d) Leonardo da Vinci

505.

Which is a novel by Margaret Mitchell published in 1936?
a) *Gone with the Wind*
b) *Wuthering Heights*
c) *A Tale of Two Cities*
d) *White Fang*

506.

Who was the famous aviator whose plane was lost near Howland Island in the Pacific in 1937?
a) Orville Wright
b) Amelia Earhart
c) Charles Lindbergh
d) none of the above

507.

Who was one of the greatest American poets of the 19th Century?
a) Walt Whitman
b) e e Cummings
c) Robert Frost
d) Allen Ginsberg

508.

When Jackie Robinson joined the Brooklyn Dodgers in 1947, what did he accomplish?
a) he was the youngest player ever in the league
b) he established a union for players
c) he broke the record for number of home runs
d) he broke the color barrier in Major League Baseball

509.

Painter Thomas Sully is famous for which work of art?

a) *Promenade*
b) *Gloucester*
c) *Sugaring-off*
d) *Washington's Crossing of the Delaware*

510.

Norman Rockwell is best known for his work on the covers of which journal?

a) *New Yorker*
b) *Saturday Evening Post*
c) *The New York Times*
d) none of the above

511.

Near which sea were scrolls that contained writings from the Old Testament found?

a) the Black Sea
b) the Dead Sea
c) the Red Sea
d) the Caspian Sea

512.

Which play written by Henrik Ibsen is about a woman who wants to establish a life of her own?

a) *The Awakening*
b) *The Golden Notebooks*
c) *A Doll's House*
d) *Fear of Flying*

513.

What is Haiku?
a) a blessing conferred when someone sneezes
b) a form of Japanese poetry
c) a small mammal
d) none of the above

514.

What group featured Smokey Robinson?
a) Twisters
b) Marvels
c) Miracles
d) Sensations

515.

What is known as Pablo Picasso's landmark work?
a) *Guernica*
b) *La Celestina*
c) *Woman With a Fan*
d) *Lady in Blue*

516.

Which Greek tragedy did Sophocles write?
a) *Oedipus Rex*
b) *Antigone*
c) *Electra*
d) none of the above

517.

Which actress won an Academy Award for these movies: *Gone with the Wind* and *A Street Car Named Desire*?
a) Vivien Leigh
b) Olivia de Havilland
c) Bette Davis
d) Myrna Loy

518.

An artwork that exaggerates features humorously is referred to as a
a) cartoon
b) caricature
c) casting
d) portrait

519.

Which form of music is not a style of rock and roll?
a) Heavy Metal
b) Disco
c) New Wave
d) Swing

520.

Where did the poet Homer come from?
a) Spain
b) Paris
c) Greece
d) Germany

521.

In which city did the story of the famed novel *The Hunchback of Notre Dame* take place?
a) St. Petersburg
b) Leon
c) Paris
d) Orleans

522.

Who founded the religion of Islam?
a) Jesus
b) Buddha
c) Mohammed
d) Gandhi

523.

Where is a famous celebration of Mardi Gras held each year?
a) St. Louis
b) Detriot
c) New Orleans
d) Dallas

524.

Where do monks live?
a) monastery
b) cloister
c) convent
d) inner sanctum

525.

Why was Brown vs the Board of Education of Topeka a landmark case?

a) it led to the Supreme Court ruling that segregation in public schools was unconstitutional

b) it prohibited prayer in public schools

c) it allowed teachers of both sexes equal pay

d) none of the above

526.

Which movie was a silent film?

a) *The Island*

b) *The Birth of a Nation*

c) *Man in the Gray Flannel Suit*

d) *Yankee Doodle Dandy*

527.

For which movie did Bette Davis win an Academy Award for Best Actress?

a) *Jezebel*

b) *The Little Foxes*

c) *A Pocketful of Miracles*

d) *Now Voyager*

528.

When did the Challenger space shuttle disaster take place?

a) 1980

b) 1983

c) 1986

d) 1990

529.

Originally, to which branch of the Armed Forces did the Air Force belong?
a) Navy
b) Marines
c) Army
d) Coast Guard

530.

Who was Horatio Alger?
a) an American novelist
b) a fictional character
c) an inventor
d) none of the above

531.

In 1775, in one of the first battles of the American Revolution, who—along with the Green Mountain Boys—took Fort Ticonderoga from the British?
a) Ethan Allen
b) Thomas Jefferson
c) George Washington
d) Nathan Hale

532.

In ballet, how many positions are there for the feet?
a) 3
b) 4
c) 5
d) 6

533.

In which decade were the Twist and the Pony popular social dances?
a) 1940s
b) 1950s
c) 1960s
d) 1970s

534.

Which Chilean poet was also its ambassador to France?
a) Pablo Neruda
b) Vincente Huidobro
c) Niconor Parra
d) Gabriela Mistral

535.

In which movie starring Joan Crawford did Clark Gable star as an escaped convict?
a) *Strange Cargo*
b) *Spy Hunt*
c) *In Harm's Way*
d) *The Enforcer*

536.

To whom are fables with animals that teach a moral lesson attributed?
a) Plato
b) Dante
c) Aesop
d) Aristotle

537.

Which famous story is from a collection entitled *1001 Arabian Nights?*
a) Aladdin and the Magic Lamp
b) Ali Baba and the Forty Thieves
c) The Enchanted Horse
d) all of the above

538.

Which is true of these books: *The Good Earth*, *The Old Man and the Sea*, and *Beloved?*
a) all were written in the 1950s
b) all won the Pulitzer Prize in Literature
c) all were written by men
d) none of the above

539.

Where in the world is the world's most comprehensive museum of air and space exploration?
a) Washington, D.C.
b) Paris, France
c) Helsinki, Finland
d) Chicago, Illinois

540.

Who can "turn the world on" with her smile?
a) That Girl
b) Ally McBeal
c) Mary Richards
d) Peggy Fleming

541.

Which was not a chief of the Apaches?
a) Geronimo
b) Cochise
c) Vitorio
d) Sitting Bull

542.

How many leagues are there in baseball?
a) one
b) two
c) three
d) four

543.

Which character from L. Frank Baum's *The Wizard of Oz* went to the Wizard for a brain?
a) Dorothy
b) Lion
c) Tin Man
d) Scarecrow

544.

According to proper etiquette, how would you address the Pope if you met him in person?
a) Your Holiness
b) Your Excellency
c) Father
d) Sir

545.

All Quiet on the Western Front is a
a) movie about World War II
b) a novel about World War I
c) a guide book to California
d) the memoirs of Lewis and Clark

546.

Which is the largest bear in the world?
a) black bear
b) polar bear
c) panda bear
d) Kodiak Bear

547.

What name did Marlon Brando call out in a famous scene from the movie version of *A Streetcar Named Desire*?
a) Mary
b) Stella
c) Angie
d) Pattie

548.

Where is Harvard University located?
a) Boston
b) Pennsylvania
c) New York City
d) Philadelphia

549.

Which are the Prairie Provinces of Canada, the second largest country in the world?
a) Ontario
b) Alberta
c) Saskatchewan
d) Manitoba

550.

Where does Congress meet to make the laws of the United States?
a) the Lincoln Memorial
b) the Washington Monument
c) the White House
d) the U.S. Capitol Building

551.

Which sea surrounds the northern coast of South America?
a) Caspian Sea
b) Mediterranean Sea
c) Caribbean Sea
d) Black Sea

552.

Which is the only deer where both the male and female have antlers?
a) mule deer
b) whitetail deer
c) reindeer
d) none of the above

553.

Who was the first U.S. president to appear on television?
a) Franklin D. Roosevelt
b) John F. Kennedy
c) Harry S. Truman
d) Dwight D. Eisenhower

554.

In which decade did the Great Depression occur?
a) 1920s
b) 1930s
c) 1940s
d) none of the above

555.

Which animal builds a home called a lodge?
a) seal
b) beaver
c) turtle
d) snake

556.

According to proper etiquette, how would you address a king or queen if you met him or her in person?
a) Your Grace
b) Your Majesty
c) Your Excellency
d) Your Eminence

557.

What role did Sissy Spacek play in the movie based on the life of Loretta Lynn?
a) a farmer's daughter
b) a minister's daughter
c) a coalminer's daughter
d) none of the above

558.

In which classic story does a young girl fall down a rabbit hole?
a) *Alice's Adventures in Wonderland*
b) *Alice Doesn't Live Here Anymore*
c) *Alice Through the Looking Glass*
d) none of the above

559.

Who is famous for his beloved fairy tales?
a) Alan King
b) Jacques Costeau
c) Harry Andersen
d) Hans Chrstian Andersen

560.

In 1954, who won the Nobel Prize in Literature?
a) Herman Melville
b) Eugene O'Neill
c) Tennessee Williams
d) Ernest Hemingway

561.

Who won the Nobel Prize in Literature in 1953?
a) Winston Churchill
b) William Faulkner
c) Albert Camus
d) Ernest Hemingway

562.

Who wrote the line "Happy families are all alike, every unhappy family is unhappy in its own way"?
a) Grimm
b) Tolstoy
c) Dickens
d) Molière

563.

Who played the first feature film *Batman?*
a) Michael Keaton
b) Val Kilmer
c) George Clooney
d) Christopher Reeve

564.

Which is the second largest continent in the world?
a) Africa
b) North America
c) India
d) Greenland

565.

For how many nights did the queen of legend,
Scheherazade, tell her husband stories?
a) 1000
b) 1001
c) 2000
d) 2001

566.

Was Phileas Fogg a
a) philosopher
b) fictional character
c) pilot
d) sea captain

567.

Which was the first U.S. earth satellite launched into
orbit in 1958?
a) Explorer 1
b) Vanguard
c) Pioneer 4
d) Telstar

568.

Which book, published in 1962, helped launch the
environmental movement in the U.S.?
a) *Silent Spring*
b) *The Secret Garden*
c) *I Never Promised You a Rose Garden*
d) *Silent Thunder*

569.

What were the 1920s known as?
a) Age of Innocence
b) Roaring Twenties
c) New Era
d) Depression

570.

Which is the longest suspension bridge in the U.S.?
a) Verrazano Narrows Bridge
b) Golden Gate Bridge
c) Brooklyn Bridge
d) George Washington Bridge

571.

Which band was lead by singer Jim Morrison?
a) The Doors
b) The Animals
c) The Flying Burrito Brothers
d) The Outlaws

572.

What is the 0 degree line of latitude on the globe called?
a) tropic of cancer
b) equator
c) tropic of Capricorn
d) prime meridian

573.

For which religion is the Ganges River sacred?
a) Taoism
b) Buddhism
c) Hinduism
d) Judaism

574.

When was Thurgood Marshall elected to the U.S. Supreme Court to become the first African-American named to such a post?
a) 1967
b) 1956
c) 1972
d) 1984

575.

In Judaism, at what age does a boy mark the beginning of his adulthood or religious responsibility?
a) 13
b) 14
c) 15
d) 16

576.

Finish the proverb, Discretion is...
a) the better part of valor
b) hard to come by
c) sacred
d) more valuable than wisdom

577.

Which U.S. president had a sign on his desk that read, "The buck stops here"?
a) Lincoln
b) Johnson
c) Truman
d) Eisenhower

578.

Who do some people believe was the real author of Shakespeare's plays?
a) Christpher Marlowe
b) Francis Bacon
c) Charles Dickens
d) Samuel Beckett

579.

Which is the process of sterilizing liquids to kill bacteria by using heat?
a) oxygenation
b) homogenization
c) pasteurization
d) sterilization

580.

In the proverb, what is the best teacher?
a) prosperity
b) health
c) experience
d) commerce

581.

Whose name is commonly associated with playing by or keeping to the rules?
a) Doyle
b) Hoyle
c) Boyle
d) Royle

582.

What were dinosaurs—the great lizards that perished 65 million years ago?
a) amphibians
b) reptiles
c) mammals
d) none of the above

583.

Which phrase means created for a particular occasion?
a) ad hoc
b) adieu
c) admit
d) adjourn

584.

Percival Lowell, a U.S. astronomer, spent many years observing and mapping which planet?
a) Venus
b) Mars
c) Pluto
d) Mercury

585.

What was the greatest paleontological discovery of anthropologists Louis and Mary Leakey?
a) the skull of homo habilis
b) the Dead Sea Scrolls
c) Atlantis
d) the jaw of homo sapiens

586.

Which emperor of China did Marco Polo — a traveller and merchant — work for for many years?
a) Kublai Khan
b) Genghis Khan
c) Aga Khan
d) Shah of Iran

587.

Adieu, adios, and auf wiedersehen all mean
a) hello
b) come again
c) good-bye
d) welcome

588.

Who was Ann Margret's boyfriend in the movie Bye, Bye Birdie?
a) Frankie Avalon
b) Paul Anka
c) Bobby Rydell
d) Troy Donahue

589.

Montezuma was ruler of the Aztecs when which explorer invaded his kingdom?
a) Pizarro
b) Columbus
c) Cortes
d) Magellan

590.

Who was one of the most famous American frontiersmen?
a) Nathaniel Hawthorne
b) Daniel Boone
c) Paul Bunyan
d) Miles Standish

591.

The FBI is the law enforcement arm of
a) Dept. of Commerce
b) Dept. of Transportation
c) Dept. of Justice
d) Internal Revenue Service

592.

How did Daniel Boone become a national hero in 1784?
a) he published a book about his adventures
b) he established a new colony
c) he defeated an Indian chief
d) he defended Plymouth colony

593.

Which movement in literature stressed expressing emotions and being free from rules?
a) Romanticism
b) Classicism
c) Existentialism
d) Nihilism

594.

Who was Don Quixote's sidekick?
a) Pancho Villa
b) Sancho Panza
c) Sonny Corleone
d) Santa Ana

595.

What is the break between factions of a church called?
a) schism
b) prism
c) clash
d) divide

596.

Who, in 1902, sang the songs on the first record to ever sell over one million copies?
a) Enrico Caruso
b) Franco Corelli
c) Franz Volker
d) Miguel Fleta

597.

Erich Weiss was the real name of which one of these beloved magicians?
a) David Copperfield
b) Harry Houdini
c) Lance Burton
d) Harry Blackstone

598.

Which movie was not directed by Cecil B. DeMille?
a) *Ben Hur*
b) *Samson and Delilah*
c) *The King of Kings*
d) *The Ten Commandments*

599.

What is the name of a ceremonial trumpet used on Rosh Hashanah and Yom Kippur?
a) Shofar
b) dreidle
c) yamulke
d) Shabbat

600.

In which century was *The Three Musketeers* written by Alexandre Dumas?
a) 16th
b) 17th
c) 18th
d) 19th

601.

Who danced with Gene Kelly in the film musical
An American in Paris?
a) Cyd Charisse
b) Ginger Rogers
c) Leslie Caron
d) none of the above

602.

In 1679, which city was the first to hire fire fighters?
a) Providence
b) New York
c) Boston
d) Philadelphia

603.

Which is not a vertebrate?
a) fish
b) human
c) bat
d) octopus

604.

What is the U.S. flag popularly known as?
a) the Great Seal of the U.S.
b) the Red, White and Blue
c) the Stars and Stripes
d) the Standard Bearer

605.

What was the motto of the The Three Musketeers?
a) No man is an island.
b) All for one and one for all.
c) Ask not what your country can do for you.
d) To be or not to be.

606.

Who was the first inquisitor general of the Spanish Inquisition?
a) Torquemada
b) Quasimodo
c) Voltaire
d) Gauguin

607.

In which year did *The Lost Weekend*, starring Ray Milland, win the Academy Award for Best Picture?
a) 1945
b) 1950
c) 1955
d) 1960

608.

Which famous historical figure was the Bloody Mary cocktail named after?
a) Mary I, Queen of England
b) Typhoid Mary
c) Mary O'Reilly
d) Mary Stewart

609.

In which decade did *Gigi*, *Ben-Hur*, and *Around the World in Eighty Days* win Best Picture of the Year awards?
a) 1940s
b) 1950s
c) 1960s
d) none of the above

610.

During which season of the year is Ramadan celebrated?
a) summer
b) spring
c) fall
d) winter

611.

In the hit song performed by Dionne Warwick, how does this question end: Do you know the way to...
a) San Juan
b) San Jose
c) San Luis Obispo
d) San Pedro

612.

What is "It's only a drop in the bucket" an example of?
a) a cliche
b) poetry
c) alliteration
d) allusion

613.

What is the name for singing without the accompaniment of musical instruments?

a) aria
b) solo
c) a cappella
d) open mic

614.

What is the name for the prize given at the Academy Awards ceremony held once a year in Hollywood?

a) Felix
b) Oscar
c) Emmy
d) Grammy

615.

What is a piece of music for one voice in opera called?

a) aria
b) duet
c) solo
d) instrumental

616.

Who went from playing TV's Remington Steele to playing James Bond?

a) Roger Moore
b) Timothy Dalton
c) Pierce Brosnan
d) Bruce Willis

617.

When was the first African-American woman elected to Congress?
a) 1960
b) 1963
c) 1968
d) 1972

618.

Which U.S. president was the first to visit Moscow and who was distinguished for helping forge a landmark strategic arms pact with Russia?
a) Richard Nixon
b) Jimmy Carter
c) Gerald Ford
d) Ronald Reagan

619.

Who was the first player to break the season record set by Roger Maris by hitting 62 home runs?
a) Reggie Jackson
b) Sammy Sosa
c) Mark McGwire
d) Joe DiMaggio

620.

Which Biblical personage is considered to be the founding patriarch of Judaism?
a) Adam
b) Saul
c) Abraham
d) Moses

621.

According to the 10th edition of the Merriam Webster's
Collegiate Dictionary, which three will be added as
new entries?
a) feng shui
b) bioregion
c) portobello
d) massive

622.

On which space shuttle did John Glenn—the first U.S.
astronaut to orbit earth—return to space in the 1990s?
a) Discovery
b) Challenger
c) Explorer
d) Adventure

623.

In which state is the National Park with the largest
known caverns?
a) Colorado
b) Utah
c) New Mexico
d) Montana

624.

Who immortalized the screen legend Bette Davis with
the best-selling song of 1981?
a) Neil Diamond
b) Natalie Cole
c) Tina Turner
d) Kim Carnes

625.

What is an eponym?
a) words that have a similar meaning
b) a word that has the same meaning as another
c) a word that has two meanings, but is spelled the same
d) a word named for a person

626.

What does the word apropos mean?
a) relevant
b) reticent
c) recipient
d) none of the above

627.

What does the phrase "c'est la vie" mean?
a) way to go
b) what will be will be
c) that's life
d) seize the day

628.

Who was the world renowned trumpet player and entertainer known as Satchmo?
a) Neil Armstrong
b) Louis Armstrong
c) George Armstrong Custer
d) Thelonious Monk

629.

When did Panama take control of the Panama Canal?
a) December 31, 1999
b) December 31, 1998
c) December 31, 1996
d) January 1, 1999

630.

In which popular TV show did Bruce Willis star with Cybil Shephard?
a) *Moonlighting*
b) *Remington Steel*
c) *L.A. Law*
d) *Dynasty*

631.

Who is the current Prime Minister of Great Britain?
a) Tony Blair
b) John Major
c) Margaret Thatcher
d) Harold Wilson

632.

When did Neil Armstrong take the first step on the moon?
a) July 1969
b) May 1968
c) October 1969
d) July 1970

633.

From which movie did the phrase "May the force be with you" come?
a) *Indiana Jones*
b) *Star Wars*
c) *The Godfather*
d) *Prizzi's Honor*

634.

During which of his inaugural addresses did President Franklin Delano Roosevelt say, "The only thing we have to fear is fear itself"?
a) first
b) second
c) third
d) fourth

635.

By what name was Charles the Great also known?
a) Charles the Bold
b) Charles the Fearless
c) Charlemagne
d) Chanticleer

636.

When did Eli Whitney invent the cotton gin?
a) 1793
b) 1693
c) 1893
d) 1905

637.

Which National Park features underground caves and a 300-foot river below the surface?
a) Denali National Park, Alaska
b) Hawaii Volcanoes, Hawaii
c) Bighorn Canyon, Wyoming
d) Mammoth Caves, New York

638.

Which is the most visited site in the U.S. National Parks system as of 1998?
a) Blue Ridge Parkway
b) Lake Mead
c) Statue of Liberty
d) Grand Canyon

639.

In which movie based on a Jules Verne story did Pat Boone play an important role?
a) *Fantastic Island*
b) *Journey to the Center of the Earth*
c) *Around the World in Eighty Days*
d) *Twenty-thousand Leagues Under the Sea*

640.

Who invented the lightning rod in 1752?
a) Ben Franklin
b) Marconi
c) Isaac Newton
d) Edmond Halley

641.

Who devised the formula $E=mc^2$?
a) Albert Einstein
b) Albert Switzer
c) Edward Teller
d) J. Robert Oppenheimer

642.

Which acclaimed novel did George Orwell write in 1948?
a) *1984*
b) *Fahrenheit 451*
c) *A Clockwork Orange*
d) *Stranger in a Strange Land*

643.

The words cold and hot, little and big are examples of
a) synonyms
b) antonyms
c) contractions
d) none of the above

644.

Who said "Genius is 1% inspiration and 99% perspiration"?
a) Thomas Edison
b) Ben Franklin
c) Alexander Graham Bell
d) Mark Twain

645.

When he rubs a magic lamp, a genie appears to grant three wishes
a) Peter Pan
b) Ali Baba
c) Aladdin
d) Jack

646.

Who coached the Green Bay Packers to victory in the first and second Super Bowl Games?
a) Vince Lombardi
b) Bill Parcells
c) Pat Riley
d) Tom Landry

647.

Which is a book that tells the story of a person's life?
a) biography
b) autobiography
c) memoir
d) all of the above

648.

Who said "That's one small step for man, one giant leap for mankind"?
a) Neil Armstrong
b) John Glenn
c) Monty Hall
d) Buzz Aldrin

649.

When the boy cried wolf one too many times, what happened?
a) everyone came running
b) no one listened to him
c) his mother punished him
d) he lost his voice

650.

Who played Marlon Brando's sister-in-law in the movie *A Streetcar Named Desire?*
a) Claire Bloom
b) Jane Fonda
c) Janet Leigh
d) Vivien Leigh

651.

Which patriotic song is the National Anthem of the U.S.?
a) America
b) My Country Tis of Thee
c) The Star-Spangled Banner
d) The Battle Hymn of the Republic

652.

Who drove the runaway bus in the movie *Speed*, starring Keanu Reeves?
a) Meg Ryan
b) Sandra Bullock
c) Lisa Kudrow
d) Gwyneth Paltrow

653.

In which large stadium were competitions held between warring gladiators?

a) Colosseum

b) Acropolis

c) Parthenon

d) none of the above

654.

Which of the figures from mythology ruled Fire?

a) Hermes

b) Hades

c) Uranus

d) Poseidon

655.

Where is the Eiffel Tower?

a) London

b) Madrid

c) Paris

d) Brussels

656.

Who invented the motorcycle?

a) Daimler

b) Mitsubishi

c) Ford

d) Harley Davidson

657.

When was the ball point pen invented?
a) 1688
b) 1788
c) 1888
d) none of the above

658.

In the lullaby, if the mockingbird don't sing what will papa bring?
a) a new bird
b) a diamond ring
c) a bottle of milk
d) a pacifier

659.

In computer terms, download means?
a) transfer a copy of a file from one computer to another
b) print
c) receive a message
d) turn off computer

660.

What is the biggest celebration held at the White House annually?
a) New Year's Soiree
b) the Easter Egg Hunt
c) Christmas tree lighting
d) Fourth of July

661.

Which enormous stone structure was erected by the ancient Egyptians?
a) Stonehenge
b) Easter Island monuments
c) the Sphinx
d) Washington Monument

662.

Which is the largest state of the U.S.?
a) California
b) New York
c) Alaska
d) Rhode Island

663.

Which is an active volcano in the U.S.?
a) Mount Washington
b) Mount Ranier
c) Mount St. Helens
d) Mount McKinley

664.

In computer terms, FAQ means?
a) facts, answers, queries
b) facts and questions
c) frequently asked questions
d) a frequency level

665.

Who was the second man to walk on the moon during the first such event in history?
a) David R. Scott
b) William A. Anders
c) Edwin "Buzz" Aldrin, Jr.
d) Neil Armstrong

666.

What is Tammy Wynette's advice in her hit song?
a) Stand By Me
b) Give Me A Call
c) Stand By Your Man
d) Go Away

667.

What is the name of the U.S. Naval Academy?
a) West Point
b) The Citadel
c) Annapolis
d) none of the above

668.

Which animals live in groups called colonies?
a) fish
b) ants
c) bees
d) beavers

669.

What is the study of ancient peoples known as?
a) paleontology
b) anthropology
c) archaeology
d) sociology

670.

Which is the most popular auto race in the U.S.?
a) Le Mans
b) Daytona 500
c) Indianopolis 500
d) Grand Prix

671.

In computer terms, mouse means
a) an arm rest
b) a unit of information
c) a pointing device
d) a keyboard

672.

How many stories does the Sears Tower in Chicago have?
a) 80
b) 60
c) 110
d) 45

673.

Who was the founder of the American Red Cross?
a) Clara Wheeler
b) Clara Barton
c) Catherine Barton
d) Carla Wheelwright

674.

Where is the home of Baseball's Hall of Fame?
a) Los Angeles
b) Cooperstown
c) Philadelphia
d) Charleston

675.

In 1895, who invented the wireless high-frequency telegraph?
a) Marconi
b) Eastman
c) Fermi
d) Edison

676.

What does .com designate on the Internet?
a) a commercial or business organization or company
b) a military organization
c) a non-profit organization
d) an international organization

677.

What formula unlocked the secrets of the atom?

a) $e=mc^2$

b) $p=\dfrac{RA}{l}$

c) $s=v+$

d) $F^2=xy$

678.

In what year did acts of Congress establish Puerto Rico and Hawaii as U.S. territories?

a) 1900

b) 1901

c) 1902

d) 1899

679.

Who wrote the book *Silent Spring* that helped launch the environmental movement?

a) Rachel Field

b) Rachel Carson

c) Ralph Nader

d) Carson McCullers

680.

In 1974, who broke Babe Ruth's career record for homeruns?

a) Hank Aaron

b) Ted Williams

c) Jackie Robinson

d) Cy Young

1. **(d)** New Hampshire
2. **(d)** Mickey Mouse
3. **(b)** Amelia Earhart
4. **(a)** baseball
5. **(a)** Hannibal
6. **(b)** an earthquake
7. **(d)** Wyatt Earp
8. **(a)** Antony and Cleopatra
9. **(a)**, **(b)**, and **(c)** Carrera, Pavarotti, and Domingo
10. **(c)** the bald eagle
11. **(a)** omega
12. **(d)** Realism
13. **(b)** Thomas Edison
14. **(d)** Eva Marie Saint
15. **(d)** Duke Ellington
16. **(b)** Florida
17. **(a)** New York Yankees
18. **(b)** the heart
19. **(a)** Florida
20. **(b)** Gulf of Mexico

21. **(a)** the first baby born in America to English parents in 1587
22. **(d)** all of the above
23. **(a)** Friendship 7
24. **(a)** the brain
25. **(c)** Mr. President
26. **(a)** the Bible
27. **(d)** Wayne Gretzky
28. **(a)** Salem, Massachusetts
29. **(c)** *It Happened One Night*
30. **(b)** Abraham Lincoln
31. **(b)** geyser
32. **(b)** Art Garfunkel
33. **(a)** Boston Harbor
34. **(b)** Richard Rogers
35. **(b)** hummingbird
36. **(a)** George Washington was named commander-in-chief
37. **(c)** England
38. **(b)** Philadelphia

39. **(b)** a famous outlaw

40. **(b)** Miranda v. Arizona

41. **(a)** New York Yankees

42. **(a)** basketball

43. **(a)** John Adams

44. **(d)** the first book was printed in America

45. **(d)** Miss Vicki

46. **(d)** all of the above

47. **(a)** Bjørn Borg

48. **(c)** popular card games

49. **(a)** Steffi Graf

50. **(a)** muscles

51. **(a)** bowling

52. **(a)** skeleton

53. **(a)** Bette Davis

54. **(a)** marsupialia

55. **(b)** *Moby Dick*

56. **(a)** juvenile

57. **(a)** Michael Jordan

58. **(a)** Roe v. Wade

59. **(a)** the first woman to race in the Indianapolis 500

60. **(c)** Greece

61. **(c)** 14

62. **(c)** Charles W. Fairbanks

63. **(b)** Katherine Switzer

64. **(c)** Roger Williams founded Providence, Rhode Island

65. **(a)** jet engine

66. **(a)** the color of the skin

67. **(b)** teenage girls

68. **(c)** Grimsby

69. **(c)** omega

70. **(a)** Billie Jean King

71. **(b)** the Garden of Eden

72. **(c)** Mount Ararat

73. **(d)** speech

74. **(a)** the Gold Rush

75. **(a)** Leonardo da Vinci

76. **(c)** The Declaration of Independence was approved

77. **(b)** *The Searchers*

78. **(a)** Andy Warhol

79. **(d)** Seurat

80. **(b)** 1950s

81. **(a)** Michigan

82. **(b)** a pair of
contradictory words

83. **(d)** a drop in
the bucket

84. **(a)** *On the Road*

85. **(b)** Rossini

86. **(a)** shall inherit
the earth

87. **(b)** Michelangelo

88. **(a)** an ethical teaching

89. **(a)** Montana

90. **(c)** Kentucky

91. **(b)** a muralist

92. **(a)** Corinthian

93. **(c)** 1940s

94. **(a)** fire

95. **(a)** Realism

96. **(a)** Nautilus

97. **(b)** Paul Henreid

98. **(a)** down the lane

99. **(a)** air, gas

100. **(b)** Modern Age

101. **(b)** Hawaii

102. **(a)** Little Big Horn

103. **(b)** NAACP

104. **(a)** the first woman
governor in the U.S.
in 1925

105. **(a)** Shirley Chisholm

106. **(d)** 1999

107. **(a)** vaccines

108. **(a)** Jamestown, Virginia

109. **(a)** Erie Canal

110. **(b)** all played Scrooge

111. **(a)** Ireland

112. **(b)** his grin

113. **(a)** magma

114. **(a)**, **(c)** and **(d)** Vasco
da Gama, Ferdinand
Magellan, and
Bartholomeu Dias

115. **(b)** Edgar Allan Poe

116. **(b)** The Ugly Duckling

117. **(a)** Pacific

118. **(c)** Belgium

119. **(d)** glass slipper

120. **(c)** two

121. **(b)** Atlantic

122. **(a)** Arizona

123. **(d)** all of the above

124. **(c)** Brussels

125. **(b)** one of straw

126. **(d)** the Black Death

127. **(a)** the Stonewall
Rebellion

128. **(a)** Harriet Tubman

129. **(d)** all of the above

130. **(c)** Liberace

131. **(a)** Vassar College

132. **(b)** James Cook

133. **(d)** early Europeans

134. **(b)** crash

135. **(a)** parts of the Sistine
Chapel

136. **(a)** Ray Bradbury

137. **(a)** a pharaoh

138. **(c)** the Red Sea

139. **(c)** *The Old Man and
the Sea*

140. **(d)** Mother's Day

141. **(a)** great virtues

142. **(b)** Orson Welles

143. **(b)** *Washington Post*

144. **(c)** a military
organization

145. **(a)** bale

146. **(a)** Thanksgiving Day

147. **(b)** Revelation

148. **(b)** *Moby Dick*

149. **(c)** Elton John

150. **(a)** was the first woman
astronaut to travel
in space

151. **(c)** age

152. **(c)** Jefferson Airplane

153. **(c)** Warhol

154. **(a)** Matthew, Mark, Luke
and John

155. **(a)** City of Peace
156. **(d)** an international organization
157. **(c)** just kidding
158. **(c)** Surrealism
159. **(b)** Charlie Chaplin
160. **(b)** by the way
161. **(b)** Sandra Day O'Connor
162. **(a)**, **(c)**, and **(d)** Baroque, Georgian, and Gothic
163. **(c)** M
164. **(c)** Janet Reno
165. **(a)** 6
166. **(a)** Vermont and Kentucky
167. **(a)** the galaxies believed to be nearest to the Milky Way
168. **(b)** France
169. **(b)** *Cow's Skull*
170. **(b)** Egypt

171. **(a)** and **(c)** an olive branch and a dove
172. **(b)** a non-profit organization
173. **(a)** chemistry
174. **(a)** Egypt
175. **(a)**, **(b)**, and **(c)** alti-, cerebro-, and demi-
176. **(d)** Walt Whitman
177. **(a)** China
178. **(c)** ta ta for now
179. **(a)** canopy
180. **(a)** photojournalist
181. **(b)** wisdom
182. **(c)** Louisa May Alcott
183. **(c)** Adams
184. **(a)** Asia
185. **(b)** Indian
186. **(c)** for your information
187. **(a)** Eureka!
188. **(a)** strength
189. **(b)** Tonto
190. **(a)** Belgium

191. **(a)** Mountain Time

192. **(a)** proverb

193. **(b)** cheepers

194. **(b)** Hans Christian Andersen

195. **(a)** Spain

196. **(a)** Charles Dickens

197. **(b)** Industrial Revolution

198. **(a)** the South

199. **(a)** one

200. **(b)** the Pyrennes

201. **(a)** garnet

202. **(a)** Joan of Arc

203. **(a)** Quetzalcoatl

204. **(b)** the Alamo

205. **(a)** Florence Nightingale

206. **(b)** Carnegie

207. **(a)** Cetacea

208. **(b)** 4

209. **(c)** equinox

210. **(b)** Elizabeth Arden

211. **(b)** Mother Teresa

212. **(c)** James Stewart

213. **(c)** Buffalo Bill Cody

214. **(a)** major holidays of Judaism

215. **(a)** ruby

216. **(c)** China

217. **(a)** Johann Gutenberg

218. **(c)** primates

219. **(a)** Louis Pasteur

220. **(a)** Ivan Pavlov

221. **(b)** Nelson Rockefeller

222. **(a)** murder

223. **(a)** Marie Curie

224. **(b)** Tom Hanks

225. **(a)** Siddhartha

226. **(a)** emerald

227. **(b)** sleuth

228. **(a)** in a flower

229. **(c)** oxygen

230. **(c)** Mary

231. **(d)** Charlotte Brontë

232. **(a)** mispell

233. **(a)** all are from California
234. **(c)** Bobby Darin
235. **(a)** Pythagoras
236. **(a)** England
237. **(b)** cubs
238. **(a)** Monet
239. **(b)** *Leave It to Beaver*
240. **(a)** Egyptians
241. **(b)** Central Time
242. **(a)** the World Cup Women's Title Game
243. **(a)** Excelsior!
244. **(b)** John Elway
245. **(a)** New York Knicks
246. **(d)** all of the above
247. **(a)** the 12th Earl of Derby
248. **(c)** Florida
249. **(d)** Appalachian Spring
250. **(b)** Austria
251. **(a)** Pearl Harbor
252. **(a)** apprise

253. **(a)** New York Yankees
254. **(d)** *A Hard Day's Night*
255. **(a)** with praise
256. **(a)** *Bolero*
257. **(b)** words
258. **(a)** Aaron Copland
259. **(a)** *Le Nozze di Figaro*
260. **(b)** an apple
261. **(b)** *Yellow Submarine*
262. **(a)** by the sun's rays at Olympia in Greece
263. **(a)** Wayne Gretzky
264. **(a)** Terrell Davis
265. **(a)** morning glory
266. **(a)** every two years
267. **(b)** $\bar{M}$
268. **(a)** Germany
269. **(a)** Phil Esposito
270. **(b)** Cleveland
271. **(a)** word for word
272. **(a)** Susan B. Anthony
273. **(b)** *The Great Gatsby*
274. **(a)** *All the President's Men*

275. **(a)** Show Me State

276. **(a)** all are famous Arizonans

277. **(c)** Atlanta Braves

278. **(b)** Puccini

279. **(a)** *Turandot*

280. **(a)** Thriller

281. **(c)** change his spots

282. **(b)** the French and Indian War began

283. **(b)** Herman Melville

284. **(c)** Florida

285. **(b)** Alzheimer's Disease

286. **(b)** diabetes

287. **(a)** and **(b)** *William Tell* and *The Barber of Seville*

288. **(a)** Giuseppe Verdi

289. **(a)** a music professor

290. **(a)** $\overline{V}$

291. **(a)** IX and X

292. **(c)** greenhouse effect

293. **(b)** acid rain

294. **(a)** North America

295. **(a)** all are toothless mammals

296. **(b)** change your mind constantly

297. **(a)** a backbone

298. **(a)**, **(b)**, and **(c)** Cretaceous, Jurassic, and Triassic

299. **(a)** *Uncle Tom's Cabin*

300. **(a)** play music quickly

301. **(d)** Alicia Alonso

302. **(a)** *The Turning Point*

303. **(c)** *The Hurricane*

304. **(a)** Thurgood Marshall

305. **(a)** the Boston Tea Party

306. **(b)** the Bible

307. **(b)** the most direct route

308. **(d)** a mischief maker

309. **(a)** Aloha State

310. **(b)** Orson Welles

311. **(d)** Mark Rothko

312. **(c)** Abstract Expressionism

313. **(a)** Pierre and Marie Curie

314. **(d)** Leonard Bernstein

315. **(a)** a picture

316. **(c)** XIII and XIV

317. **(a)** Chuck Noll

318. **(a)** theory of relativity

319. **(b)** San Francisco 49ers

320. **(b)** necessity

321. **(c)** can keep it free of charge

322. **(a)** Holland

323. **(a)** France

324. **(a)** Immigration and Naturalization Service

325. **(a)** promote assistance among worldwide police authorities

326. **(a)** you've found something you've been looking for

327. **(b)** *The Night of the Hunter*

328. **(b)** *How Green Was My Valley*

329. **(a)** iota

330. **(a)** palindrome

331. **(c)** fiction

332. **(a)** Sumerians

333. **(b)** *An American in Paris*

334. **(d)** epic poem

335. **(a)** face to face

336. **(a)** a program designed for a specific task

337. **(b)** you're in trouble for something

338. **(b)** 1970s

339. **(a)** Gwyneth Paltrow

340. **(d)** Buffalo Bills

341. **(b)** are managing the best you can with the resources at hand

342. **(a)** a new constellation

343. **(a)** South Dakota

344. **(c)** William Holden

345. **(c)** fencing

346. (b) a wolf in sheep's clothing

347. (b) become comfortable in a situation

348. (d) *Woman with Chrysanthemums*

349. (a) *Water Lilies*

350. (b) Burt Bacharach

351. (b) ante mezzo

352. (b) complain constantly about the same thing

353. (b) taken a nap or slept

354. (b) thank you

355. (b) RSVP

356. (a) the Middle Ages

357. (a) you've changed your mind

358. (d) Classicism

359. (c) rose

360. (a) *Point Break*

361. (a) the 4th Earl of Sandwich

362. (a) New York, N.Y.

363. (a) Poseidon

364. (a), **(b)**, and **(c)** Apollo, Ares, and Dionysus

365. (c) easy as pie

366. (d) heart

367. (c) the other way around

368. (b) Abraham and his descendants

369. (a) Babel

370. (a) Geneva Convention

371. (a) Ben Franklin

372. (b) maintain world peace and security

373. (b) Centennial Exposition

374. (d) alkaline battery

375. (b) IBM

376. (a) *West Side Story*

377. (c) Achilles

378. (b) love

379. (b) Amazons

380. (a) Andrew Johnson

381. (a) tenpins

382. (a) to move the ball down the field and across the goal line into the opponent's end zone

383. (a) his heel

384. (c) the first theater opened in the colonies in Williamsburg, Virginia

385. (a) true

386. (b) *Ed Sullivan Show*

387. (b) Venus

388. (a) George Washington was elected to be the first president

389. (b) *Star Trek*

390. (c) Camelot

391. (b) 1854

392. (a) Steffi Graf

393. (a) beauty

394. (a) Czech Republic

395. (c) Zeus

396. (a) sailor

397. (a) Auld Lang Syne

398. (a) rock and jazz

399. (c) Chris Evert

400. (a) he took the sword Excalibur out of a stone

401. (b) the Golden Fleece

402. (a) the peacock

403. (a) Artemis

404. (a) the Pony Express

405. (c) Clint Eastwood

406. (a) protects it from the sun's rays

407. (a) Far East and India

408. (c) Middle Ages

409. (a) pretty ugly

410. (c) letters from the Hebrew alphabet

411. (a) brain

412. (a) an enchantress

413. (b) *Mission Impossible*

414. (a) Avalon

415. (a) Appomattox Court

House, Virginia

416. (a) Buffalo

417. (c) Panama Canal opened

418. (b) astrology

419. (a) low-lying cities would flood

420. (c) Sir Lancelot

421. (b) James Cook

422. (b) Marilyn McCoo

423. (a) Athena

424. (b) Athena

425. (c) the Hole in the Wall Gang

426. (b) never the twain shall meet

427. (a) water

428. (c) Odysseus

429. (d) Atlantic Ocean

430. (c) Pegasus

431. (b) Africa

432. (b) United States

433. (b) Maria

434. (b) Sears Tower

435. (c) Sahara

436. (c) the coronation of Queen Elizabeth II

437. (b) France

438. (b) when you are playing golf

439. (b) *Moby Dick*

440. (b) Victor Fleming

441. (b) Seneca

442. (b) North Sea

443. (c) a hummingbird

444. (b) Georgia

445. (b) Sir Arthur Conan Doyle

446. (a) illness was not caused by evil spirits

447. (b) he dropped objects from the Leaning Tower of Pisa

448. (c) Nemesis

449. (b) Francis Bacon

450. (c) genuine imitation

451. (b) Middle Ages
452. (a) 1915
453. (c) physics
454. (b) that man
455. (a) they completed the first transcontinental telephone call
456. (b) King Arthur
457. (b) Ernest Hemingway
458. (b) Victor Fleming
459. (a) Renaissance
460. (b) Atlas
461. (b) Beauty and the Beast
462. (c) start up your computer
463. (d) failure of a program or a disk
464. (a) backward
465. (c) Romeo and Juliet
466. (a) compact disk read-only memory
467. (b) Pacific Time

468. (d) ballroom dances
469. (d) Africa-Cuba
470. (b) Sonny and Cher
471. (a) Thomas Edison
472. (b) 6
473. (c) Babe
474. (b) Northern U.S. and Canada
475. (a) New York Islanders
476. (c) The Spirit of St. Louis
477. (a) Pearl Buck
478. (a) both reigned in "Camelot"
479. (a) *Ninth Symphony*
480. (d) Rachmaninoff
481. (a) Bhagavad Gita
482. (b) blue whale
483. (c) Georges Bizet
484. (a) the Fonz
485. (a) the state of total peace
486. (b) Shakespeare
487. (c) *Tamburlaine*

488. (c) Harold Pinter

489. (b) Miguel de Cervantes

490. (c) El Cid

491. (d) all of the above

492. (a) types of whales

493. (c) Johann Bach

494. (a) Igor Stravinsky

495. (a) play music slowly

496. (c) *Where the Wild Things Are*

497. (a) China

498. (b) 1800

499. (a) Montreal Canadiens

500. (b) George M. Cohan

501. (c) Cyrillic

502. (c) Clint Eastwood

503. (d) Anton Chekov

504. (c) Seneca

505. (a) *Gone With the Wind*

506. (b) Amelia Earhart

507. (a) Walt Whitman

508. (d) he broke the color barrier in Major League baseball

509. (d) Washington's Crossing of the Delaware

510. (b) *Saturday Evening Post*

511. (b) the Dead Sea

512. (c) *A Doll's House*

513. (b) a form of Japanese poetry

514. (c) Miracles

515. (a) *Guernica*

516. (a) *Oedipus Rex*

517. (a) Vivien Leigh

518. (b) caricature

519. (d) Swing

520. (c) Greece

521. (c) Paris

522. (c) Mohammed

523. (c) New Orleans

524. (a) monastery

525. (a) it led to the Supreme Court ruling that segregation in public

schools was
unconstitutional

526. (b) *The Birth of a Nation*

527. (a) Jezebel

528. (c) 1986

529. (c) Army

530. (a) an American
novelist

531. (a) Ethan Allen

532. (c) 5

533. (c) 1960s

534. (a) Pablo Neruda

535. (a) *Strange Cargo*

536. (c) Aesop

537. (d) all of the above

538. (b) all won the Pulitzer
Prize in literature

539. (a) Washington, D.C.

540. (c) Mary Richards

541. (d) Sitting Bull

542. (b) two

543. (d) Scarecrow

544. (a) Your Holiness

545. (b) a novel about World
War I

546. (d) Kodiak bear

547. (b) Stella

548. (a) Boston

549. (b), **(c)**, and **(d)** Alberta,
Saskatchewan, and
Manitoba

550. (d) the U.S. Capitol
Building

551. (c) Caribbean Sea

552. (c) reindeer

553. (a) Franklin D. Roosevelt

554. (b) 1930s

555. (b) beaver

556. (b) Your Majesty

557. (c) a coalminer's
daughter

558. (a) *Alice's Adventures in
Wonderland*

559. (d) Hans Christian
Andersen

560. (d) Ernest Hemingway

561. (a) Winston Churchill
562. (b) Tolstoy
563. (a) Michael Keaton
564. (a) Africa
565. (b) 1001
566. (b) fictional character
567. (a) Explorer 1
568. (a) *Silent Spring*
569. (b) Roaring Twenties
570. (a) Verrazano Narrows Bridge
571. (a) the Doors
572. (b) equator
573. (c) Hinduism
574. (a) 1967
575. (a) 13
576. (a) the better part of valor
577. (c) Truman
578. (b) Francis Bacon
579. (c) pasteurization
580. (c) experience
581. (b) Hoyle

582. (b) reptiles
583. (a) ad hoc
584. (b) Mars
585. (a) the skull of homo habilis
586. (a) Kublai Khan
587. (c) good-bye
588. (c) Bobby Rydell
589. (c) Cortes
590. (b) Daniel Boone
591. (c) Dept. of Justice
592. (a) he published a book about his adventures
593. (a) Romanticism
594. (b) Sancho Panza
595. (a) schism
596. (a) Enrico Caruso
597. (b) Harry Houdini
598. (a) *Ben Hur*
599. (a) Shofar
600. (b) 17th
601. (c) Leslie Caron
602. (c) Boston

603. **(d)** octopus
604. **(c)** the Stars and Stripes
605. **(b)** All for one and one for all
606. **(a)** Torquemada
607. **(a)** 1945
608. **(a)** Mary I, Queen of England
609. **(b)** 1950s
610. **(b)** spring
611. **(b)** San Jose
612. **(a)** cliche
613. **(c)** a capella
614. **(b)** Oscar
615. **(a)** aria
616. **(c)** Pierce Brosnan
617. **(c)** 1968
618. **(a)** Richard Nixon
619. **(c)** Mark McGuire
620. **(c)** Abraham
621. **(a)**, **(b)**, and **(c)** feng shui, bioregion, and portobello

622. **(a)** Discovery
623. **(c)** New Mexico
624. **(d)** Kim Carnes
625. **(d)** a word named for a person
626. **(a)** relevant
627. **(c)** that's life
628. **(b)** Louis Armstrong
629. **(a)** December 31, 1999
630. **(a)** *Moonlighting*
631. **(a)** Tony Blair
632. **(a)** July 1969
633. **(b)** *Star Wars*
634. **(a)** first
635. **(c)** Charlemagne
636. **(a)** 1793
637. **(d)** Mammoth Caves, N.Y.
638. **(a)** Blue Ridge Parkway
639. **(b)** *Journey to the Center of the Earth*
640. **(a)** Ben Franklin
641. **(a)** Albert Einstein
642. **(a)** *1984*

643. **(b)** antonyms

644. **(a)** Thomas Edison

645. **(c)** Aladdin

646. **(a)** Vince Lombardi

647. **(d)** all of the above

648. **(a)** Neil Armstrong

649. **(b)** no one listened to him

650. **(d)** Vivien Leigh

651. **(c)** the Star-Spangled Banner

652. **(b)** Sandra Bullock

653. **(a)** Colosseum

654. **(b)** Hades

655. **(c)** Paris

656. **(a)** Daimler

657. **(c)** 1888

658. **(b)** a diamond ring

659. **(a)** transfer a copy of a file from one computer to another

660. **(b)** the Easter Egg Hunt

661. **(c)** the Sphinx

662. **(c)** Alaska

663. **(c)** Mount St. Helens

664. **(c)** frequently asked questions

665. **(c)** Edwin "Buzz" Aldrin, Jr.

666. **(c)** Stand By Your Man

667. **(c)** Annapolis

668. **(b)** ants

669. **(c)** archaeology

670. **(c)** Indianapolis 500

671. **(c)** a pointing device

672. **(c)** 110

673. **(b)** Clara Barton

674. **(b)** Cooperstown

675. **(a)** Marconi

676. **(a)** a commercial or business organization or company

677. **(a)** $e=mc^2$

678. **(a)** 1900

679. **(b)** Rachel Carson

680. **(a)** Hank Aaron